MURDER IN THE FRONT ROW

HARALD OIMOEN & BRIAN LEW

Bazillion
Points

METALLUS MAXIMUS PRODUCTIONS PRESENTS

METALLICA
METAL UP YOUR ASS

"METAL MONDAZE"
OLD WALDORF
OCT. 18TH

APPEARING ON THE COMPILATION ALBUM
"METAL MASSACRE" ON METAL BLADE RECORDS

FOR METALLICA DETAILS: METALLICA, 345 W. RIVERSIDE DR.,
ROSEBURG, OREGON 97470 OR (714) 640-2799

THE MANIACS RETURN!!!
METALLICA
METAL UP YOUR ASS
OLD WALDORF
MON. NOV. 29
SPECIAL GUESTS: VICIOUS RUMOURS & EXODUS

FOR METALLICA DETAILS: METALLICA, 345 W. RIVERSIDE DR.,
ROSEBURG, OREGON 97470 OR (714) 640-2799

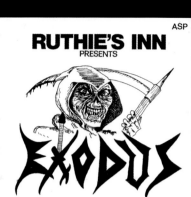

ASP

RUTHIE'S INN
PRESENTS

EXODUS

WITH
VICIOUS RUMORS
AND
TEMPTRESS

FRI MAR 30TH 9PM

2618 SAN PABLO, BERKELEY

BORN TO MUTILATE
AND THAT'S ALL
IT IS!!

MEGADETH

RATTLE
YOUR FUCKIN
BRAINS
OUT

FAST...LOUD...AND RUDE!

FEB.17th   FEB.19th
BERKELEY, CA.   SAN FRANCISCO
RUTHY'S INN   THE STONE
2618 San Pablo Ave. 412 Broadway
(415) 849-3258   (415) 391-8282

BACK TO MARAUD!

LIVE FOR METAL - DIE FOR....
MEGADETH

THEIR
CONVENTICLE
GATHERS
AT/ON

A
P
R.

KEYSTONE
BERKELEY
15

PALO
ALTO
16

S.F.
18

THE MEGADETH FAN CLUB
438 Joshua Way
Sunnyvale, California 94086

TICKETS ON SALE
AT BASS OUTLETS
FOR SHOW INFO.—
(415) 391-8292/10239

FAST... LOUD...
AND RUDE!
IN-STORE APPEARANCE AT THE RECORD VAULT!
APRIL 18 NO WIMPS!

HEAVY METAL SPECIAL
FROM L.A.
MEGA-DETH
WITH
DAVID MUSTAINE
EX-METALLICA
PLUS
TROUBLE
FROM CHICAGO

ALSO
AVATTOR
FROM LA

RUTHIES FRI. FEB. 17TH
2618 SAN PABLO

5$
TICKETS AT BASS

KEYSTONE BERKELEY PRESENTS
"THE BAY AREAS HEAVIEST"

EXODUS

WITH....
SABATOGE
PLUS.... HELL METAL GUESTS !!......
MACHEN ASSAULT !

WED. AUG 3RD (BE THERE & BANG)!

METALLUS MAXIMUS PRODUCTIONS PRESENTS
THE HEAVIEST NIGHT OF YOUR LIFE!
WITH
METALLICA
METAL UP YOUR ASS
FROM
SEATTLE **CULPRIT** AND SPECIAL GUESTS **WARNING**
THE STONE
SAT MARCH 19 9:00
412 BROADWAY S.F.

LAST BAY AREA APPEARANCE BEFORE EAST COAST TOUR AND ALBUM RELEASE
METALLIBANGER INFO: METALLICA, 345 W. RIVERSIDE DR., ROSEBURG, OR. 97470-(415) 524-8333

SKULL SPLITTING
METAL!!!

MEGADETH

FAST...LOUD...AND RUDE!

FEB.17th   FEB.19th
BERKELEY, CA.   SAN FRANCISCO
RUTHY'S INN   THE STONE
2618 San Pablo Ave. 412 Broadway
(415) 849-3258   (415) 391-8282

PLUS
SCREAMING FROM L.A.!!!

ABATTOIR

P.O. BOX 3612, ALHAMBRA, CA 91803

THE RETURN OF

SLAYER

RUTHIES INN   KEYSTONE
BERKELEY   PALO ALTO
MARCH 17   MARCH 19
SAN PABVE.
2618 SAN PABLO AVE.   260 CALIFORNIA PALO ALTO
415-849-3258   415-324-1402

Clear & Distinct Ideas & GOLDENVOICE
MIND-FRYING METAL
VENOM
SLAYER
EXODUS
SUNDAY, APRIL 14
SAN JOSE
CIVIC AUDITORIUM
BASS TICKETRON 7:00 PM

ASP
RUTHIE'S INN
PRESENTS
A RAGING METAL ATTACK
FEATURING
THE HEAVIEST BAND IN THE WORLD
EXODUS
WITH
BLIND ILLUSION
AND
TEMPTRESS
PLUS
SPECIAL GUESTS
BLIZZARD
SAT APR 14TH 9PM
2618 SAN PABLO, BERKELEY

Miller MUSIC PLAYED THE AMERICAN WAY
New Year's Eve
BILL GRAHAM PRESENTS
METALLICA
EXODUS
METAL CHURCH · ANTHRAX
Tuesday, December 31, 8PM
San Francisco Civic
Tickets: $20 advance
TICKETS AVAILABLE AT ALL BASS TICKET CENTERS
CHARGE BY PHONE: 415/762-BASS

SLAYER
EXODUS
POSSESSED
VERMIN
SATURDAY-6-23
RUTHIES INN

NORTHERN CALIFORNIAS ONLY APPEARANCE
FEB. 21, 1986, 8:00
AT THE SALINAS COMMUNITY CENTER
CHAMPION PRODUCTIONS
PRESENTS

WITH GUEST
D.R.I.
$13.50 BASS, TICKETRON, SHERWOOD HALL
$14.50 AT THE DOOR
DONT MISS IT!!!
NORTHERN CALIFORNIAS ONLY APPEARANCE

LEGACY DEATH ANGEL
- AND -
I SAID, WE'RE NOT PROMOTING VIOLENCE, WIMP!!
Dec 3
7 pm
BAM
$4
SAN FRANCISCO
THE STONE
412 BROADWAY

SPASTIC CHILDREN
featuring METALLICA members
with guest Violence & Betrayal
Friday, January 2, 1987. 7:00p.m. $6.00
ROCK ON BROADWAY, 435 broadway, frisco

THE ULTRA-VIOLENCE
RECORD RELEASE
GIG!
DEATH ANGEL
WITH
MORDRED

PLACE - THE STONE
DATE - MAY 12
TIME - CURFEW 7:00
SPRING SALE
$6

EXPERIENCE THE
GENOCIDAL MAYHEM OF
LEGACY
BLIND ILLUSION
AND
VIOLENCE
SAT. SEP. 28TH
AT RUTHIE'S INN! 9:00 PM
2618 San Pablo Berkeley

MACHO HEMAN SHOW
ONLY $5.00
SPASTIK CHILDREN
Forn Krah Krell Tour
PAUL BALOFF'S
MADLE!
CURFEW
PILLAGE
W/ SUNDAY
7:00 P.M.
TUES. AÜG. 16
THE STONE S.F.

EASTERN FRONT
AQUATIC PARK
3RD & BANCROFT WAY, BERKELEY
12 NOON TIL 7 PM

SATURDAY, AUG. 18	SUNDAY, AUG. 19
CIRCLE JERKS	SUICIDAL TENDENCIES
BEASTY BOYS	EXODUS
JERRY'S KIDS (BOSTON)	SLAYER
F.U.'S (BOSTON)	BLUE CHEER
O.T.B.A.	ROAD RUNNER
	O.T.B.A.

SATURDAY, AUG. 25	SUNDAY, AUG. 26
SUN RA	(COUNTRY BAR B QUE)
CARRIBEAN ALLSTARS	JOHN LEE HOOKER
LOOTERS	HEARTS ON FIRE
HIEROGLYPHICS	MUD DOGS
NEW BREED	SNAPPERS
O.T.B.A.	WILD GAME
	O.T.B.A.

ADVANCE TICKETS AT BASS

LEGACY
MORDRED
AND
SACRILEGE
WED. MAY 27TH ALL AGES 7:45 PM
AFTER THIS SHOW LEGACY WILL BE KNOWN AS TESTAMENT

KRQR AND THE OLD WALDORF
PRESENT THE HELL METAL PARTY FEATURING

LAAZ ROCKIT
METALLICA
SPECIAL METAL GUESTS
IMPORTED FROM L.A.
OCTOBER 18TH METAL MONDAY 8 PM
OLD WALDORF 444 BATTERY ST., S.F.
SPECIAL OPENING METAL ACT
Laaz Rockit would like to thank all the loyal Headbangers who have made playing in the Bay Area feel so great "Keep on Banging"

MURDER IN THE FRONT ROW:
Shots From the Bay Area Thrash Metal Epicenter

Third printing 2017 by

Bazillion Points

Bazillion Points
New York
United States
www.bazillionpoints.com
www.murderinthefrontrow.com

Produced for Bazillion Points by Ian Christe

Copyediting by Polly Watson
Production by Magnus Henriksson
Cover layout and design by Bazillion Points
Additional photos, artifacts, and lightning by John Marshall, Tim Healy, Doug
Goodman, Rich Hosey, John Scharpen, and Wayne Vanderkuil

A bazillion thank-yous to Calumet Photographic, Christine Park, Ron Quintana, Gary
Holt, Alex Skolnick, Robb Flynn, Monte Conner, Dianna Dilworth, Vivi, and Roman.

ISBN 978-1-935950-03-5

Printed in China

Facing page and previous overleaf: *Crowd clusters.* HARALD OIMOEN. Front endpapers: *Slayer, Aquatic Park, August 19, 1984.* HARALD OIMOEN; *Kerry King, blood upon the stage.* HARALD OIMOEN. Back endpapers: *The indestructible Toby Rage flies over a Slayer show.* HARALD OIMOEN; *Exodus, Aquatic Park, Berkeley, August 19, 1984.* BRIAN LEW.

Clockwise from top: *Ozzy Osbourne and Randy Rhoads, Diary of a Madman tour, Cow Palace, SF, December 30, 1981.* HARALD OIMOEN; *Metallica secret Day on the Green warm-up show, Ruthie's Inn, Berkeley, August 24, 1985.* UNKNOWN; *The night Lars Ulrich met Slayer, the Kabuki Theater, April 12, 1985* HARALD OIMOEN

I WASHED DISHES FOR METALLICA

by Harald Oimoen

Well . . . this is it! You hold in your hands the culmination of a lifelong dream for me. When Brian Lew and I took all these shots back in the day, little did we know the true historical significance they would have, twenty-five-plus years later. We had *no idea* how big all of our friends in Metallica, Slayer, Megadeth, Exodus, and the others would become. We were just kids who totally *loved* metal and pretty much lived and breathed it 24/7.

The early '80s was an exciting time to be a metalhead living in the SF Bay Area, let me tell ya! In the pre–Internet/eBay/Amazon world, we really had to hunt and search all over the place for the latest metal albums and cassettes (this was also the pre-CD world). This hunt is what I like to refer to as "the Quest." We had a hard time finding anything *heavy* and *metal* because these things were was so new and underground. Growing up in the San Jose, California, suburb of Sunnyvale, I had to venture to bigger cities like San Francisco and Berkeley to find anything cool. We were hungry for anything fast, obnoxious, and brutal! Little did we suspect that the fastest, heaviest riffs ever were about to hit us right in the jaw—delivered by bands in our very own backyard.

Then the dam began to burst. (Were you wearing denim? Were you wearing leather?) The NWOBHM started happening—the New Wave of British Heavy Metal, for the few uninitiated out there. Tons of cool new metal bands came popping out of the woodwork! First and foremost was Iron Maiden, with their twin guitar harmonies and almost punkish vocals of Paul Di'Anno. Their mascot Eddie was the coolest *ever*. Then Motörhead, Angel Witch, Raven, Venom, Saxon, and even the first couple Def Leppard albums totally blew our young, impressionable minds. I'll never forget hearing Accept's "Fast as a Shark" for the first time. This was pretty much considered the fastest, heaviest thing we had heard up to that point. Thank God for specialty metal shops like the Record Vault in SF, where we found all the latest metal releases; literature like the UK's metal bible, *Kerrang!*; plus patches, badges, and a plethora of metal goodies. I used to go on huge shopping sprees at the Vault—especially after I traded a bunch of my shots for credit in the store.

Metal music grew way more fast, heavy, and extreme, as a bunch of cool bands from Europe started popping up, like Mercyful Fate, Kreator, and Celtic Frost. The first time I heard Mercyful Fate's *Nuns Have No Fun* EP, I didn't know it was a 45-rpm record—I played it at 33 rpm. Just imagine how strange King Diamond's weird falsetto sounded when slowed way down to the wrong speed!

Around this time, I started meeting lots of like-minded metal enthusiasts, like Rich "Banger" Burch. Rich told me on one of our many quests that if we were lucky we'd find a *Kerrang!* magazine—and sure enough, we did, a major score. Rich was a totally devoted Motörheadbanger who would travel all over the Bay Area with his *huge* oversize boom box on his shoulder, making unsuspecting pedestrians jump ten feet when he would blast anything he thought was heavy. His quote on the back cover of Metallica's *Kill 'Em All* reads, Bang That Head That Doesn't Bang, which is exactly what he would say and do to people at gigs who weren't headbanging! He would come up behind them and violently force their heads up and down while screaming that now classic catchphrase in their ears!

Rich turned me on to countless killer bands, and he introduced me to KUSF DJ and *Metal Mania* zine editor Ron Quintana, who was *the* metal guru dude with the hugest collection of new amazing demo and live tapes I had ever seen. I started taking photos, and Rich insisted that I contribute my shots to Quintana's hilarious, groundbreaking, and irreverent fanzine. I'll never forget reading Ron's amazingly prophetic line about Metallica. Very early on, he wrote that they had "potential to become U.S. metal gods!" Holy right-on predictions, Batman!

Another like-minded kid I met was fellow headbanging photographer Brian Lew, also a huge tape trader in contact with people all over the world. We always bumped into each other while snapping photos up front at all the heaviest local club gigs. We were both especially fond of

From top: *Bay Area bangers at a Savatage gig, 1985.* UNKNOWN; *Harald O. and Cliff Burton, Aquatic Park, Berkeley, August 19, 1984.* UNKNOWN; *Harald O. with Lars Ulrich, August 1985.* UNKNOWN

the up-and-coming local band Y&T, who were absolutely incredible live back then (before wimping out horribly!) At the time, Y&T were like our own personal little local secret that we loved, that we didn't wanna share with the rest of the world. It was a similar feeling later on, when Metallica started getting huge in Europe, way before the States.

Brian was the first guy to introduce me to Metallica, both musically and personally. I cannot overstate how crucial he was in helping me join the band's inner circle at such an early stage, making possible all the photos that eventually sprang out of it. One of the coolest things about Metallica in particular was the great friendship we developed with the band, which continues to this day. I always tripped on how cool it was to actually become pals and drinking partners with one of my fave bands ever. They were just some buddies of ours who just so happened to be in *the heaviest band in the world*! I was so friggin' stoked that I had my foot in the door. Brian eventually drifted away before coming back with a vengeance. But I was set!

Metallica were absolutely *on fire* back then, and so crushing live! Cliff was incredible to photograph; he had such a cool and original stage presence, headbanging at half the speed of the rest of the band. I thought James looked so cool onstage with his bullet belt, black spandex pants, and red sleeveless shirt that I was impressed enough to adopt a similar stage image for myself in my band. I searched high and low for a similar Smirnoff shirt to no avail. Lingerie specialists Frederick's of Hollywood was the only place I knew of that sold black spandex, and it was really embarrassing shopping there!

In the beginning, James Hetfield was totally shy. Maybe that was why there were no cameras allowed at one show at the Stone in 1983. I had to sneak my camera in, which I became pretty good at over the years. I got popped by security, though, and they took my camera away. Luckily I was able to rewind the film back into the canister before they opened the back and exposed it. I got the roll of film back thanks to Cliff Burton going to bat for me.

I became pals with all the other heaviest bands of the day, like Megadeth, Slayer, Suicidal Tendencies, plus shredding speed metal punkers Verbal Abuse, Fang, C.O.C., and in particular D.R.I.—who played so much faster and punkier than anything I had ever heard. Exodus also built quite a following with ultraviolent, out-of-control, blistering live performances that have still never been rivaled by anyone. Once the second-wave bands like Death Angel, Testament, Vio-lence, Heathen, Forbidden, and Possessed started gigging regularly, the area rapidly became one big monstrous scene, with everybody hanging out and consuming mass quantities of alcohol together on a regular

basis. It was great, everybody knew everybody else. Many times bands would play all three Keystone Clubs. I would usually go to the Keystone Palo Alto and remain somewhat sober so I could concentrate on taking photos. Then the following night at the Stone in Berkeley, I would concentrate more on slamming, moshing, and getting drunk! I still brought my camera; I was hooked—big-time!

The photo thing happened more or less organically, with me showing the bands all the shots I had taken from previous gigs. They liked my pictures enough to start pilfering them from me when we ran into each other around town, and eventually many used my photos on their albums. I wanted to be just like *Kerrang!* mainstay Ross Halfin, a British photographer whom I envied and looked up to for his killer Maiden shots. He had never even heard of Metallica in those days. I met him backstage at a Maiden show in San Jose, and he was a stuck-up jerk who refused to give a star-struck kid named Harald an autograph. Through the years, Ross has made my quest for worldwide metalliphoto domination really tough. What an ass!

In spring of 1984 I got a call from Brian that changed my life. He had just talked to Cliff Burton, who was in Denmark putting the finishing touches on Metallica's second album, *Ride the Lightning*. Brian told me Cliff wanted to use one of my shots for the back cover of the album. I couldn't friggin' believe it! One of my favorite bassists in one of my favorite, most killer bands ever, wanted to use my picture on his album. I was so stoked and excited! I got the biggest thrill in my life riding my bike to the Record Factory in Sunnyvale, picking up an import copy of *Ride the Lightning*, and seeing my shot of Cliff on the back. Words cannot explain how it felt to see my photo printed in full color on the back cover of an album. I was totally hooked! I frantically opened the record, searching for my name printed on the sleeve. I totally freaked when I saw myself listed in the special thanks list as "'Weird' Harold O." Then, separated from the LP thanks list, were the actual back cover photo credits listing the photographers who had taken each live shot, including: "CLIFF—HAROLD O."

I couldn't believe every metalhead who bought that Metallica album all over the world was going to read my name! It turned out Cliff couldn't remember how to spell my strange Norwegian last name, so he just credited me as "Harold O." Little did Metallica know, they had unwittingly given me a long-lasting new nickname. "Harald Oimoen" now became "Harald O.," and I was off and running.

I became good friends with death metal pioneers Possessed, and took on the role of semi-official band photographer, shooting all the photos on their first two albums. They had the coolest manager, a sweet friendly older lady named Debbie Abono. She became like a second mom to me and so many other people in the Bay Area, always helping bands get gigs and supporting all of us in our efforts. I even went on a few short road trips with Possessed up the coast to Washington and Oregon, supporting Slayer on their *Live Undead* tour. They asked me to go to a one-off show at L.A.'s Olympic Auditorium, where they were supporting D.R.I., C.O.C., and Anthrax, so my camera could document this killer gig for posterity.

That road trip became one of the scariest, most dangerous, and nerve-wracking episodes of my life. The adventure started out innocently, with a Possessed in-store appearance at a really cool little metal record shop in L.A. The band signed ceramic skulls. Jeff Becerra, Mike Torrao from Possessed, and I also received gold pentagram necklaces as gifts. Unfortunately, they were cursed, and set in motion a chain of events that chill me to the bone to this day! After that in-store, things started going horribly wrong. Mike Torrao's amps blew out mysteriously as Possessed started its set, cutting the band's stage time to a measly twenty minutes. Then, during the second song, the barricade collapsed on me while I was taking shots down in the photo pit, pinning my leg against the stage and crushing it with the weight of the entire huge unruly crowd behind me! If I hadn't seen the collapse coming out of the corner of my eye, I would have been crushed to death.

Finally, the crowd backed up enough for me to extract my badly injured leg from the battered barricade, and I collapsed onstage in front of Jeff Becerra. He stopped the show immediately and called for help. I was carried offstage and brought to an office where the two sleazebag promoters told me my leg wasn't bad and that I would be okay. I stupidly believed them, and went hobbling off to shoot photos of D.R.I. and C.O.C.! Eventually, while stumbling around on my broken leg, I found Debbie Abono. By then my knee had started swelling up with blood, and I started feeling faint due to my body going into shock. Meanwhile, Jeff Becerra was jumped outside by some Latino gang, and his nose was broken in the melee. Debbie attempted to drive us to a hospital, but then the curse struck again; we got a flat tire on the way to the hospital! An ambulance picked us up, but it died on the side of the road—we had to wait for another one. What was going on? Talk about a cursed trip.

Eventually we made it to the hospital, and Debbie insisted that we throw our cursed pentagram necklaces out the window. Nothing bad happened to anyone else—only Torrao, Becerra, and I had horrible things happening, and we were the only ones wearing the necklaces. This scared the crap out of me! Debbie waited on me hand and foot while I recuperated at her house. I eventually had knee surgery, and a huge piece of chipped bone was removed

through a hole drilled in my kneecap. I used to think satanism was something of a joke; now I was relieved to be alive. And it got freakier: our van odometer read 000666 when we arrived home! (Okay, I admit that part might be a little embellished.)

One of the most disappointing aspects of my photography has been getting dicked on photo credits. Case in point: Exodus's now legendary debut, the thrash classic masterpiece *Bonded by Blood.* The album's initial release was delayed a year due to problems with the artwork and so on. The anticipation for its eventual release was huge! A cassette of the album leaked, and just about everybody I knew who was into metal had a copy of it. Paul Baloff described the LP jacket to me as a painting of Siamese twin babies—one obviously evil, and the other one obviously good, trying to rip apart from his malevolent conjoined twin. I couldn't imagine what the hell this would look like! Finally the big day arrived. I rushed down to a little record shop and there it was. The cover wasn't really evil looking at all—it was actually pretty cheesy. I turned the cover over and was psyched to see three of my live shots on the back. I pulled out the sleeve and about 75 percent of the shots were mine. Killer! But I was completely crushed when I saw Exodus had totally left my name off the credits and the special-thanks list. Aaargh!

It's bad enough to not get paid a penny for shots— even more painful was the fact that *Bonded* ended up becoming a legendary thrash metal classic and nobody knew those were my photos! I was devastated. Then it happened again. Slayer did the same thing on *Hell Awaits*; but to Slayer's credit they actually had my name added on subsequent pressings, which is unheard of after an album is already released.

Slayer was of a different breed than Metallica and Megadeth. For starters, they seemed to embrace their image more. But though they were an L.A. band, they played up here at least three or four times a year. I remember them sound-checking once at the Keystone Palo Alto, and the huge intimidating club owner, Bob Corona, told them to turn down their amps. They told him to *fuck off!* Then they loaded up their gear and split back home to Los Angeles. They did not mess around!

Kerry King used to write funny little satanic sayings on all his autographs—stuff like: "Hell awaits evil souls like ours!" He wore a little button that said: DEAD PEOPLE ARE COOL. I used to help him put on his nailed armband before shows, because it was so heavy. (I always thought it would be funny to toss some oranges or tomatoes at that armband, to see if they would stick.) Once Kerry showed up unannounced out of the blue at my house in Sunnyvale. I saw somebody with long hair knocking on my front door

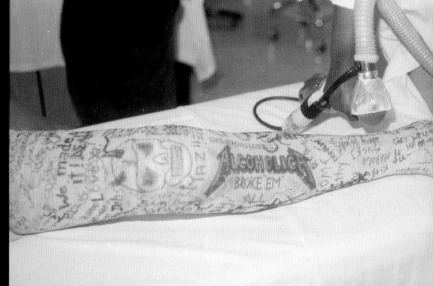

From top: *Revelers at Gary Holt's 21st birthday party, Ruthie's Inn, May 4, 1985.* UNKNOWN; *"Broke 'Em All," 1986.* UNKNOWN; *Harald O. with El Duce.* UNKNOWN

and staring at something in the bushes. He turned around, and I saw it was Kerry King! How the hell did he find my house? More importantly, what the fuck was he doing there? It turned out he wanted to see some shots I took at a Slayer show a few days before. He looked me up and found my house on a map. He was staring at the bushes because a fly had gotten stuck in a spiderweb, and he was hoping to see it be devoured. He was visibly bummed out that I answered the door before he was able to witness the fly's gruesome end. He was and is a trippy dude, way into morbid cool stuff.

One of the coolest, least known, and most unpublicized things about the Bay Area thrash metal scene back in the day has been the great camaraderie and brotherhood that was so prevalent. There was no real distinction between bands and fans like there is today. Everyone knew everybody else, and we were all one big happy, drunken, extended dysfunctional family. There was a loyal sense of community within our ranks, and everybody got along really well for the most part. On any given night you could go see Exodus, Slayer, and Possessed at Ruthie's Inn for a measly five dollars, and find yourself headbanging down front with Jaymz Hetfield, doing shots with El Duce at the bar, or hanging out at the Big O parking lot across the street, smoking a fatty with Paul Baloff. My band Terminal Shock opened for Metallica at Ruthie's Inn for about a hundred people. It was a secret benefit thing to help Ruthie's buy a new P.A. Cliff Burton and I organized the thing at the last second on the day of the show. When I told my bandmates we were opening for Metallica at Ruthie's, nobody believed me. I don't blame 'em!

The most tragic and shocking event within our close-knit scene was the death of Cliff Burton in 1986. When this happened, we were all so young that we really had no firsthand experience with death. We were completely unprepared to deal with it. This was a huge wake-up call for everyone, proving that we really weren't invincible after all (contrary to Toby Rage's inhuman feats of amazing stage diver–craft that defied gravity and all other laws of nature— see this book's cover!) The Metallicats ended up using a bunch of my Cliff photos for the home video release Cliff 'Em All. It was a thrill to see my shots on a TV for the first time, but the moment was bittersweet considering the occasion. We had all been such good friends with Cliff and were completely devastated by his untimely death.

As far as thinking we were invincible—it's totally crazy when I think how drunk and shit-faced we used to get, and how dangerous it was for us to be on the road driving. I vaguely recall driving Jaymz and Larz home from a gig, being so blind drunk that I had to fight double vision so I could focus on the road. We used to do some of the craziest, risk-

iest, most dangerous crap ever! I'm not going to go into it here; it would still freak my parents out big-time. However, I can relate one story: After yet another night of heavy booze consumption with the Metallidrunks (and there were so many), I ended up passing out on their living room couch. When I finally awoke the next day, I couldn't figure out why I was soaked with some unspeakable foul-smelling liquid material; it was all over myself and my clothes. It turned out that I had vomited in my sleep, and I easily could have ended up like Bon Scott or Jimi Hendrix, who both died from asphyxiation that way. Luckily, Jaymz had turned me on my side in the middle of the night, preventing me from dying.

I really did wash dishes for Metallica, way back in 1985, in the month preceding their hugest-ever hometown gig at Oakland Stadium for Bill Graham's Day on the Green. (For my full details on that infamous event, please refer to Joel McIver's Cliff Burton bio To Live Is to Die.) The devious Metalliteam of "Hatfield and Oilrig" concocted an ingenious scheme to mess with the O-man, yours truly. They told me they only had three photo passes for the upcoming show; if I really wanted one, I would have to earn it! I had to do their dishes, which had been sitting in the sink for days, and they had me do a variety of household chores, such as taking out the trash and performing latrine duty. I was totally duped; they were messing with me big-time and just wanted to see how far I would go to receive a hallowed D.O.G. photo pass.

Time came full circle in 2009, when Metallica invited me, Brian, and a hundred and fifty other people from their past to attend their induction to the Rock and Roll Hall of Fame. The band paid for all of us to fly to Cleveland; they put us up in a killer hotel, and the night before the induction ceremony, they threw the party to end all parties. I decided to wear a disguise just for fun, to see if I could fool any of the Metallidudes. I slicked back my hair and wore a pair of nerdy glasses, a totally fake-looking mustache, and a cheeseball leisure suit that made me look like a cheap used-car salesman from the '70s.

I sidled up to Lars Ulrich and struck up a conversation, and he had no clue who I was. "A bunch of people are supposed to be here tonight," he told me. "Brian Lew, Harald O., Ron Quintana . . ."

"Oh, reeeeeally?" I said.

He recognized me right away after that. "Fuck you, Harald!"

The rest of the night, everybody looked at me strangely due to the furry caterpillar on my upper lip, my totally crooked and obviously fake mustache. That was one of the best weekends of my life. The induction event itself was an incredibly moving affair, specifically when Cliff's father, Ray

Burton, accepted the Hall of Fame award for his son.

I am filled with utter joy, and I get kinda misty-eyed and nostalgic whenever I look back at all these photographs—shots of us growing up, almost throwing up, and becoming the people we are today! These timeless, historic shots are a cool reminder—a metal time capsule—of how pure and innocent those times were, way before it became big business. These pictures fill me with many incredible memories of so many drunken great times with so many amazing bands and friends. As the old-timers everywhere always say, if you weren't there, then you can't possibly understand! Hopefully the photos in this book have transcended that old adage by portraying the scene in such a way that younger metal enthusiasts can actually experience what it was really like to be a metalhead in the Bay Area back in the day. On this level, I think the book succeeds perfectly!!!

Today I play bass with old-school punk metallers D.R.I. We travel the world, so if you ever see us playing near your town, come on down to the show, introduce yourself, and tell me what you thought of this book! I would love to hear your thoughts and answer any questions.

From top: *Brian Lew's 19th birthday, underage drinking backstage at the Old Waldorf, SF, October 18, 1982.* UNKNOWN; *Brian Lew's bedroom wall, Sunnyvale, CA, 1983.* BRIAN LEW

by Brian Lew

Murder in the front row,
Crowd begins to bang,
And there's blood upon the stage.
Bang your head against the stage
As metal takes its price . . .
Bonded by blood.

I was at the Exodus show that inspired the song "Bonded by Blood"—it was one of the band's many nights at Ruthie's Inn in Berkeley, California. During the gig, a lot of people had left their empty drink glasses on the stage, and when Exodus commenced its mayhem some of the glasses were broken. As a result, people in the front row were cut all over their hands and arms by the broken glass, and soon the stage itself was smeared with blood. Then Paul Baloff demanded that the crowd "sacrifice a poser" to him, and the crowd obliged, throwing some hapless kid onstage. He landed at Baloff's feet, at his mercy. We were just kids having fun; sometimes the fun was violent.

I grew up listening to classic rock on Bay Area radio stations such as KOME, KJSO, KMEL, and KRQR—"The Rocker." My first concerts were big arena and stadium shows by the likes of Van Halen, Blue Öyster Cult, Black Sabbath, and AC/DC. Eventually I heard a local hard rock band called Y&T on the radio, and they became the first band I ever saw in a club, just as their *Earthshaker* album came out in 1981. At the time, Y&T were still a blue-collar area band whose members wore T-shirts and jeans onstage; this was still several years before they sold out and became hair metal wannabes. At the time, Y&T displayed a no-bullshit East Bay attitude that predated the similar attitudes of future East Bay bands such as Exodus and Machine Head. At the front of the stage at a Y&T show at the Keystone Palo Alto, I first met Harald Oimoen. We both lived in Sunnyvale, and before long we were running into each other at shows regularly, both of us with cameras in hand. Harald was (and still is!) a maniacal character. For a time, he worked at the local Photo Drive-Up in Sunnyvale, where I sometimes took my film to be developed.

My Y&T fandom drove me to seek out other under-ground hard rock and metal bands. Being a metal fan in the U.S. during the early '80s took a lot of effort. Most of the good bands and all of the good music magazines came from Europe; I gleaned all of my early metal info from the English publication *Sounds*, and then via the first issues of *Kerrang!*. The import record bin at Tower Records in Mountain View, California, changed my life; I spent almost all of my money on expensive import albums from Europe and Japan. My friend Rich Pelletier and I bought the Iron Maiden *Killers* album because the cover art was so amazing, and the band photos on the back looked so *metal*. I grew immersed in European metal and became dogmatic; I *hated* L.A. image-over-heaviness poser bands like Mötley Crüe, Ratt, and Quiet Riot. *HATED* them. My metal heroes were Iron Maiden and Motörhead, along with more underground European bands like Venom and Mercyful Fate.

Soon I was faithfully making a regular trek of over an hour from Sunnyvale up to Concord, California, to visit a record store called the Record Exchange that specialized in European metal imports. Through the Record Exchange, I became friends with other San Francisco Bay Area metal fans. I realized there were many more metal people like me out there, outside of the confines of Sunnyvale. I found a metal record store on Polk Street in San Francisco—the Record Vault—which soon became the epicenter for the original Bay Area metal scene. The Vault was a very special place, and not just because they sold all of the latest and greatest new metal. The owners were metal fans, and that passion translated into everything about the store; from the wall dedicated to Motörhead—plastered with clippings, posters, and photos of Lemmy & Co.—to the incredible in-store signing sessions they hosted with almost every major metal band of the day, including Saxon, Mercyful Fate, Venom, and, of course, Motörhead.

Even so, my limited access to the new European metal was frustrating, Of course, there was no e-mail or text messaging back then, and long distance phone calls were too expensive for a teenager like me. The only realistic way to communicate with other headbangers outside the Bay Area was by mail. Eventually I ran a pen-pal ad in *Kerrang!*. I

From top: *Iron Maiden's first Northern California appearance, Oakland Stadium, July 18, 1982.* BRIAN LEW; *Saxon, the Keystone Palo Alto, March 30, 1982. Final show of the Denim and Leather tour. Graham Oliver set his guitar on fire during the encore of "Machine Gun."* BRIAN LEW; *Bay Area heroes Y&T, aka Yesterday & Today, 1981 or 1982.* BRIAN LEW

was shocked by the avalanche of letters I received from all over the world, especially from such foreign metal strongholds as England and Holland. I started corresponding with other fans in those faraway lands. We wrote letters about shows we'd seen, sent Xeroxed copies of our tape lists, and traded concert merchandise. It took weeks, sometimes months, to communicate back and forth, but the effort was always worth it. I traded away my 1980 Van Halen and Molly Hatchet tour shirts for bounty like an Angel Witch 7" and a Girlschool 1980 tour program. Evidently the Europeans felt the same way about American rock bands as I did about their new metal bands.

Besides Europeans, I also received letters from likeminded American headbangers including Brian Slagel in Los Angeles, Ron Quintana in San Francisco, and K. J. Doughton in Roseburg, Oregon. My first published writing was a review of Metallica's first San Francisco show at the Stone on September 18, 1982, for K. J. Doughton's fanzine *Northwest Metal*. Prior to the show, K. J. had sent me Metallica's *No Life 'til Leather* demo, which he received from an L.A. tape trader named Patrick Scott. K. J. eventually ran the original official Metallica fan club from 1983 to 1987, and the joke has always been that K. J. and I were Metallica fans number five and number six. In 1982, you could literally count and name all of the band's fans that easily.

That first Metallica show changed my life. They were the first band I ever saw sound-check, the first band to put me on a guest list, and the first band to ask my opinion about things like a new song. We became friends. After that first review of mine was printed in *Northwest Metal*, Metallica returned to San Francisco to play at the Old Waldorf. I was surprised when James Hetfield introduced "Motorbreath" with something I had written in that review: "We're going to slow it down to Mach 10 for the love song. . . ." It blew my mind that a band I was fanatical about had actually read something I'd written and acknowledged it from the stage. Prior to the show, Lars had called to tell me the manager of the band Riot was going to be at the show, so could I make sure my friends and I were extra crazy during their set? I made a small sign out of cardboard that read, METALLICA FUCKING RULES, waved it around during their set, and then I threw it onto the drum riser. That show happened to fall on my nineteenth birthday, and the band dedicated "Metal Militia" to me and recorded their set for me as well. Yes, I still have that tape, and there are bootlegs of it floating around all over the place now. It was a good birthday. I don't know if Riot's manager ever really showed up or not. But months later, after Metallica had relocated to the Bay Area, I noticed my sign taped to a door inside the 3132 Carlson Boulevard house in El Cerrito, aka "the Metallica Mansion."

After befriending Ron Quintana, I contributed to his legendary fanzine *Metal Mania*, starting with a review of the debut Mercyful Fate EP on Rave-On Records. I loved Ron's sense of humor. He was ahead of his time, incorporating '60s and '70s kitsch from our childhoods in his layouts. He would print a rave review of the new Venom single, or an informative history of Uli Roth and the Scorpions; then the next page would feature some old Partridge Family trading cards. After its first seven issues, *Metal Mania* cut costs by switching from Xerox paper to cheap newsprint and cheaper ink. The local joke about every new issue was always about how much of that ink would come off on your fingers.

I eventually put out a fanzine of my own with my friend Sam Kress; we called it *Whiplash* after my favorite Metallica song. Sam was more of the business guy, as the debut issue was financed with money he had inherited. I was more the creative guy, and we worked well together. We spent a lot of time hanging out with our metalhead friends listening to metal, drinking, and being young and stupid. I can't even guess how many times I crashed on his couch instead of driving home. Before we started the fanzine, Sam went to England, where he met the managers of Venom and Mercyful Fate, as well as members of NWOBHM bands such as Blitzkrieg and Jaguar. Those became valuable contacts for us. As we were putting *Whiplash* together, Sam also traveled to New York and became friends with a guy starting a record label called Torrid. That connection led to Bay Area heroes Exodus releasing their album on the Torrid/Combat label in 1985.

The debut issue of *Whiplash* featured the first interview with James Hetfield and Lars Ulrich after they arrived in New York to record *Kill 'Em All*, plus a review of Metallica's homecoming shows on their debut U.S. tour supporting Raven. Our big coup was printing the lyrics to three unreleased new Mercyful Fate songs—"Evil," "Curse of the Pharaohs," and "Satan's Fall"—which the band's manager had given us permission to print as the issue's centerfold. The issue also featured the very first article about Megadeth, written by me; some of the very first articles anywhere about the bands Pagan Altar and Trouble; as well as interviews with Venom, Saxon, and twenty-year-old guitar prodigy Yngwie Malmsteen, who had just moved to America from Sweden. Although we did two printings of *Whiplash* #1, distributed all over North America and Europe, that was the only issue of *Whiplash* we ever published—but Sam and I had fun while it lasted. Metal was a serious calling for us, but ultimately it was all about having fun and hanging out with friends.

It's very difficult for me to articulate what that original Bay Area metal scene was like. The sense of community

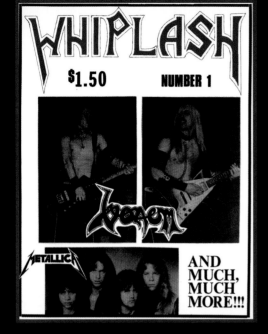

Clockwise from top left: Whiplash *number 1; Vodka raging! Brian Lew with Metallica and friends at the band's hotel after the show, November 29, 1982.* UNKNOWN; *Lars Ulrich and* Whiplash *zine cofounder Sam Kress in the lobby of Wolfgang's in San Francisco, November 18, 1983. In the background are (from left) Mark Whitaker and Dana and Leah Schecter* BRIAN LEW; *The Metallica Mansion, summer 1983. Brian Lew with James Hetfield, raging to an advance tape of* Kill 'Em All. UNKNOWN

that existed remains profound to me. Metal was a huge part of my formative years, giving me an identity when I felt isolated, and introducing me to friends when I felt lonely. When I first got into rock music in my early teens, those bands were larger than life to me. That all changed when I found the underground scene and great bands who were just regular people. There really was no distinction between the Bay Area bands and the fans. We were a big gang.

Among many great local metal bands, Exodus was the heart and soul of the original Bay Area scene. In reality, after moving here from L.A., Metallica were around for no more than six months before leaving for New York to record *Kill 'Em All*—then they were absent for most of 1983–84 during their first tours of U.S. and Europe. During this time Exodus filled the metal vacuum, and became the Bay Area metal house band. I saw Exodus twice in 1982 when Kirk Hammett was still in the band. It's funny to admit that Ron Quintana and I both thought it was Gary Holt who left to join Metallica—we didn't have their names straight, and we thought Gary was the better guitarist!

During 1983 and 1984, I saw Exodus more than twenty times as they wrote and started performing the songs that became *Bonded by Blood*. Besides many insane shows at Ruthie's Inn, two shows that stand out are Exodus's January 30, 1984, show at Wolfgang's with Slayer opening, and the Day in the Dirt outdoor show at Berkeley's Aquatic Park on August 19, 1984, with Suicidal Tendencies, Slayer, Blue Cheer, and others. Three days before the Wolfgang's show, Slayer had played their infamous first show in the Bay Area at the Keystone Berkeley. They took the stage wearing the eyeliner pictured on the photos on their first album, and some of us went to the bathroom and got paper towels and waved them at Slayer as they played, chanting: "Take off the makeup!" Needless to say, when Slayer took the stage at Wolfgang's three days later, they were not wearing eyeliner. The original Bay Area metalheads would not tolerate *any* of that L.A.-style bullshit.

While the release of Metallica's *Kill 'Em All* was huge for the Bay Area metal scene, the *Bonded by Blood* album means more to me, simply because I spent so much time around Exodus in the time leading up to its recording and release. Also, much of *Kill 'Em All* dated from Metallica's birth in Los Angeles, but Exodus and *Bonded by Blood* were completely products of the Bay Area and the East Bay: Oakland, Berkeley, Richmond, Dublin, El Cerrito, and so on. Exodus's maniacal singer Paul Baloff personified the East Bay Ruthie's Inn metal attitude, for better and for worse. He would always greet me by shouting: "BRIAN LEW!!" He never said, "Hey, man," or, "Hi Brian"—it was always "BRIAN LEW!!" in a loud, welcoming way that always made me feel part of his tribe. Baloff could be scary when

he was in full rage. Pity the foolish person who would show up at Ruthie's Inn wearing a Mötley Crüe or similar poser band T-shirt. Baloff would literally tear the shirt off that person's back because they weren't metal enough. In his words: "Metal rules! And if you don't like it, *die!*"

That intense Ruthie's Inn and East Bay environment was the perfect atmosphere for Slayer and Megadeth to cut their teeth; both bands spent a lot of time in the Bay Area and played some of their earliest shows there. I remained friends with Dave Mustaine after he "left" Metallica, and, at his request, I ran the first Megadeth fan club out of my bedroom for a short time leading up to the release of the band's debut album. Megadeth's fan club mailing address at that point was my parents' house in Sunnyvale. Though the several shows Megadeth played with Kerry King on guitar are now regarded as epic in the historic significance of the Big Four, it was cool at the time but didn't really seem like that big of a thing. Slayer and Megadeth were both new bands, after all. Back then, Brian Slagel from Metal Blade Records sent me an advance demo of Slayer's first album, *Show No Mercy*, and I played it for everybody simply because it was so much faster than Metallica. Back then all that mattered to me was how fast a band played.

Now, of course, I realize that while all of us in the Bay Area were having fun and mindlessly raging, Metallica were away from home starting their long road to becoming the biggest-selling and most successful rock band of our generation. Though they got out into the world a good amount even in those days, Metallica were always definitely part of the scene and not far from our thoughts. For example, back in 1984 when Metallica were recording *Ride the Lightning* in Denmark at Sweet Silence Studios, long distance phone calls were very expensive, especially overseas. Sam Kress and I had phone calling card numbers that were "not ours" (wink, wink), which we used to call our metal friends in faraway places. We had to do this from pay phones so the calls couldn't get traced back to us. Somehow we got word that Metallica were feeling homesick and that we should call them in Denmark to cheer them up. So one morning I drove to a local gas station to use their pay phone to call Denmark with a calling card number that was "not mine." A Danish voice answered, and I asked to speak to any of the Metallica guys. I think James came to the phone first, and I can still remember how happy his voice sounded to be receiving a call from home. I also talked to Cliff during the call—I was on that pay phone for over an hour, giving them all the news about what was going on back in the Bay Area, the best new metal demo tapes and live bootlegs being passed around, and generally bullshitting. Eventually someone tapped me on the shoulder; there were a couple of pissed-off people waiting to use pay phone! I kept the call going for a while longer, though—it wasn't every day I got to talk to my band friends in Denmark, right? During that call Cliff told me to tell Harald he wanted to use one of his photos on the cover of the upcoming new album. I told him I would tell Harald that, and I also promised to send the band some new demo and live tapes—they did get a big package of cassettes from me while they were away.

In 1986, my real life started to interfere with my metal path. I had been growing disenchanted with how big metal was getting, and how the types of people who used to be-little metal to me were suddenly listening to *my* bands and showing up at gigs. The underground element was slipping away, and I didn't like it. I went to some punk shows with my friend Wayne VanderKuil, but I couldn't fully embrace punk, because I liked heavy guitars too much! I started to listen to other genres of music altogether.

And then came September 27, 1986, which profoundly changed everything for me and my relationship with metal. It's surreal all of these years later how iconic and influential Cliff Burton has become to millions of people. When Cliff joined Metallica and played his first shows with them on March 5 and March 19, 1983, something definitely clicked with the band and they moved to another level. I feel extremely fortunate to have seen almost every Bay Area performance Cliff played with Metallica over the next three years, and I'm even more thankful to have known him.

The first time I saw and met Cliff was in March 1982, and his band Trauma was supporting Saxon at the Keystone in Palo Alto. Friends had told me I needed to see Trauma because their bass player was incredible. During their opener set, Cliff played a bass solo, which featured him using a drinking glass as a slide. A slide solo on bass at a metal show? I was blown away. I was up against the stage, and as Trauma finished I shouted at Cliff and stuck out my hand. He reached for it and shook it. Later that year, I was invited to the Carlson Boulevard house in El Cerrito where James and Lars lived—the Metallica Mansion—to see them and Dave jam with their new bassist Cliff for the first time. Metallica's discography at that point consisted of two or three demo tapes. In hindsight, the magnitude of that afternoon is pretty amazing; six other people were here with me to witness the event. The band's equipment was set up in the living room of the small two-bedroom house. The drum kit was set up in front of the couch. All of the other furniture had been cleared to make room for the amps. For most of the session I knelt on the couch behind Lars and snapped pictures with my trusty Canon AV-1. Afterward, I took the very first pictures of the band with their new bassist.

When Cliff died on September 27, 1986, metal stopped being fun for me. At the end of the day, everything

up to that point had been about having fun. I walked away from the metal scene for a while. I moved on with life and listened to non-metal music. I became friends with the bands Neurosis and the Melvins, who were then aligned with the punk scene, but who are now considered influential in the current metal scene—funny how that works. Hanging out and going on tour with those bands reminded me so much of the early Bay Area metal days. It felt like lightning had struck twice for me as I witnessed the early days of another round of influential heavy bands. I had the same experience seeing Neurosis play in a pizza parlor in Orange County in 1991 as I did seeing Metallica at the Stone in 1982: both bands were creating music that was ahead of the curve; all they needed was an audience to catch up to them.

The old metal days came full circle for me on October 12, 1991, when Metallica played a massive homecoming show at Oakland Stadium. During that day I ran into so many old friends that I hadn't seen or spoken to in years, including my former *Whiplash* partner Sam Kress. That show was like a high school reunion: I reconnected with a lot of people from the old *Bonded by Blood* days, and it was eerie how easy it was to feel part of the scene again. Since that day, I haven't been far from my old metal roots. Today I follow many of the current generation of under-ground metal bands.

The period when the original Bay Area metal scene was created was the single-most influential time period in my life. The friendships that I made back then still resonate both in my personal and professional life. I'm amazed that Harald has carried the metal torch for us all of these years, even when my interest and faith faltered! The fact that he's a member of D.R.I. now is still something I can barely wrap my head around; the first time I saw Harald play bass was in our friend Rich Pelletier's garage circa 1983 as Harald jammed with Rich's band Hellhound—the only metal band in Sunnyvale!

Finally, this book is not meant to be a definitive history book about the original Bay Area metal scene. I would pre-fer *Murder in the Front Row* to be seen as a time capsule back to the denim-and-leather times, when things were so profoundly innocent and so totally *metal*. If you were there—I hope this book reminds you of what it feels like to be young and invincible. If you weren't there—remember as you look at these photographs that the vast majority of us were just kids, under twenty-one years old when the scene started. We were just kids having fun; sometimes the fun was violent.

Bonded by blood!

Dave Mustaine, James Hetfield, and Lars Ulrich back at the hotel after Metallica's first SF show, September 18, 1982. BRIAN LEW

Cliff Burton's first Metallica rehearsal, December 28, 1982. Front row: Ian Kallen (Metal Mania), Ron Quintana (Metal Mania), Lars Ulrich, Dave Mustaine. Back row: James Hetfield, Rich Pelletier, Cliff Burton. BRIAN LEW

THIRTY YEARS AGO, MUSIC SUCKED

by Ron Quintana

Thirty years ago, music sucked. In 1981 in the Bay Area, music hella sucked. The previously vibrant San Francisco punk rock scene too quickly grew ancient and diluted, while dirty old hippie bands dominated the concert halls. Punk had been the only recent musical innovation with any balls, but it had already morphed into new wave music that sounded an awful lot like '70s disco—and that sucked. MTV had just started, but it already sucked. During Ronald Reagan's first year as president, we just had plain old bad music for boring conservative times, nothing like the crazy '60s or the hedonistic and wacky '70s. Radio really sucked. Big commercial radio everywhere has always been about dull pop pap, but the local airwaves were even worse. KSAN, the original FM free-form innovator, turned country in late 1980, which totally sucked! Only a few college and community radio stations, like KPFA, KUSF, and KALX, played any interesting music at all.

Out of this choking fog of suck emerged a throng of truly enlightened hard-rocking musicians, photographers, and fanatics not content with the status quo. These were dedicated music fans who still held out hope for something better. Heavy metal fans who had been rocking out mainly to American heavies like Van Halen, Montrose, Ted Nugent, and their ilk now began to hear strange new rumblings from the Old World. English heavy rockers—Black Sabbath, Led Zeppelin, and even Judas Priest—were already way popular. Now a whole New Wave of British Heavy Metal, the NWOBHM, came thundering forth, led by a little trio named Motörhead.

The UK music papers *Sounds*, *NME*, and *Melody Maker* diverged wildly in describing Motörhead as "heavy metal," "punk," or "the worst racket imaginable," so of course I had to hear them right away. I bought their *City Kids* EP in 1979 but ran into problems when I couldn't figure out if it sounded "right" at 33 rpm or 45 rpm. Lemmy Kilmister's voice sounded so bad, yet the band was so powerful at both speeds. That year I was eighteen, completing a boring first year at San Francisco City College. All I cared about was music. I started with the Beatles, Black Sabbath, Thin

Lizzy, and Devo, and soon was collecting every rocking record I could find, especially foreign and more extreme music. During its final year as a free-form rock beacon, KSAN broadcast tons of local concerts from its endless archives, which I recorded and traded with everyone I knew. Soon I had amassed a huge list of shows and more and more demos of metal bands from around the world by trading tapes through the mail.

Growing up in the city of San Francisco, I hung out with a group of devoted true metalheads—or Trues, as we called ourselves—who only liked the hardest-rocking bands. We always tried to outdo one another by finding the heaviest bands' records and taunting the others in our group. Each of us would race down to Recycled, Streetlight, Aquarius, or any of the other great used record stores in San Francisco and score that Riot album, Budgie 45, or—if we were really lucky—a Sabbath bootleg. Because those super-heavy bands were also the least common, we were competitive about it all. My friends whispered about "secret" stores whose whereabouts they could not divulge. Before long, the Levi's jackets of the Trues were covered in more and more obscure metal buttons and patches, just like those of the so-called headbangers we read about and saw in the pictures of the British music mags.

Being into the outer fringes of extreme music meant going to punk concerts as well as metal shows, and out of necessity most of the Trues liked punk. There was little separation of genres, as there were so few metallers anyway, and the SF punk rock scene was so huge. The infamous Mabuhay Gardens, the Mab, was ground zero for punkers, and we had at least seven or eight smaller dives around the city where we could skank, pogo, stage-dive, or crowd-walk while a dizzying array of sloppy little punk bands played. After all, in England the NWOBHM was kick-started by punk. Metal bands there were incorporating faster and shorter solos. The riffage was rougher, and the overall attitude was grittier than ever before. Heavy metal in 1981 avoided the long-winded dinosaur band sludge of the '70s. The boring old patterns had been broken and reset in the UK, and how those changes were coming out west.

But San Francisco only had a few clubs that might book small rock acts. The Old Waldorf was the only medium-size club regularly booking touring hard rock bands. Many of the Trues got jobs working there, in order to support music-collecting habits and get into the cooler gigs. Soon, a similar club opened across the street from the Mab called the Stone, with sister clubs in Berkeley and Palo Alto—the Keystones. These were much more uptight and expensive venues than the sleazy, fun Mab or comfortable Old Waldorf.

One of our circle of Trues was Rich Burch—"Skitch from Richmond"—a hard-core Motörheadaholic who introduced us to our crazy new Berkeley buddy "Pavel the Rager"—Paul Baloff. Paul first played me Motörhead's *Bomber* (on blue vinyl, no less!), the whole time screaming, "Hella heavy!" or some such East Bay phrase. Paul became a good friend, and through him the SF Trues met other East Bay ragers at gigs by Yesterday & Today (later "Y&T"), or while shopping at amazing Berkeley record stores like Rasputin or Rather Ripped. The Trues tripped up to parties in the Berkeley hills, and we'd invite the easterners over to our weekend bashes inside various city parks. Carrying giant ghetto blasters, armed with Iron Maiden or Saxon tapes, we would bring big bottles of booze or cases of beer deep into the woods or atop "Tank Hill" to avoid cops and get as loud, drunk, and rip-roaring as possible.

Our favorite spot was Strawberry Hill, in the middle of Stow Lake in darkest Golden Gate Park. That's where, one night in early 1981, I met Lars Ulrich. Rich brought this little foreign kid up to the Hill, and his denim jacket had more unusual buttons and patches than the rest of ours put together. We quizzed him on all the latest European heavies we had read or heard about, and Lars knew or had seen all of them—and many more. By coincidence, Diamond Head was my and Lars's favorite group of the moment, so he, Rich, and I talked about them and every other British band for hours that night, while Lars ended up cruising us around in his awesome green AMC Pacer.

A month later, Lars and I discovered the most hard-rocking record store: the Record Exchange, way out in Walnut Creek. To our amazement, owner Bill Burkhard had been stocking his remote suburban shop with tons of obscure NWOBHM imports unavailable previously in America. It was metal heaven! We bought vinyl LPs and 45s like Sweet Savage's "Killing Time," and I picked up the first issue of the all-metal magazine *Kerrang!*, which got me thinking about doing something similar and smaller.

Suddenly, music didn't suck anymore! In June 1981, Motörhead came to America. The super–power

trio stormed the Old Waldorf, rattling our worlds with a wickedly weighty show. They returned that July with Ozzy Osbourne's new band. Some of us waited for the band outside the Santa Cruz show, and who were the first two dudes to come off the tour bus but Skitch and Lars! They had hung out with Lemmy and company since the earlier L.A. shows, and were following our heroes around the West Coast. Most of the Trues were similarly devoted to the 'Head. To spice things up, I added photos my friends had taken of the band to my xeroxed concert tape lists. The pictures started to seem so much more interesting to me than lists of bands, so I just decided to dump the lists and begin work on a special fanzine with photos of the 'Head and my other favorite bands. I named the zine after the effect the music had on me: *Metal Mania*!

Earlier that spring, Lars and I had swapped ideas and lists of names of our possible future record store or band or magazine collaborations. I don't remember being impressed with "Lightning Vette" or other ideas on his list. I thought he liked "Skull Orchard" the best of my creations, so imagine my shock many months later when he told me he had named his new band after one of my names: "Metallica." I always felt bad about forcing that goofy name on such a naive metal dude and his friends. By August 1981 I had pasted up some good-looking photos, typed up a few pages of reviews, and completely laid out *Metal Mania* #1, featuring Motörhead. I xeroxed hundreds of copies and sold enough to pay for a second issue—and I never looked back.

In early 1982 the most amazing record store in the world opened, the Record Vault. Run by a totally dedicated family of Motörheadbangers—Pam, Zar, and Greg Smith—it became the ultimate metal destination for the remainder of the decade. The Vault carried albums, buttons, patches, posters, and concert tapes by all the significant heavies. It was everything a metalhead could ever want. I started working there, and I loved watching people's faces when they would enter the Vault for the first time. They were usually either completely bewildered, frightened, or best of all overwhelmed with joy at finding such a unique shop packed with so much metal!

On March 7, 1982, Ian Kallen, Howie Klein, and I started a Saturday night metal radio show on KUSF called *Rampage Radio*, which has continuously blasted the North Bay and East Bay every single week since that wacky first late night. We regularly assaulted listeners with our vast NWOBHM collections, along with demos and live concerts of local metallers like Anvil Chorus and then-SF-based Metal Church, plus a bevy of international crushers like Germany's Accept, Japan's Bow Wow, or Sweden's Silver Mountain.

Cliff Burton's first Metallica rehearsal, December 28, 1982. Front row: Ian Kallen, Lars Ulrich, Dave Mustaine. Back row: Ron Quintana, James Hetfield,

After many requests from its staff and customers, the Old Waldorf inaugurated its legendary "Metal Mondays" with the SF debut of Mötley Crüe in April 1982. Until then, headbangers were lucky to get a couple heavy shows per month in all of the Bay Area. Now the Waldorf was booking three or more hard-rocking acts every week. On May 3, 1982, I caught an interesting South Bay band called Trauma, featuring that unique bassist Cliff Burton plus crazy-looking guitarists with matching lightning-bolt-embossed leather outfits. That was way metal for 1982! We hung out afterward, talking to the band and the amiable cool Cliff, who was usually a friendly and fun guy to talk music with.

By then I was corresponding with two of the best local photographers in the scene: Harald Oimoen and Brian Lew. Both shared my interest in spreading the word about the heaviest bands. I begged them for hot shots for *Metal Mania*, and they contributed kick-ass pictures and much-needed reviews.

Within a few months Saxon, Girlschool, Motörhead, Krokus, Iron Maiden, Scorpions, and other Euro-metal monsters invaded America, inspiring kids in the Bay Area to start headbanging and begin bashing heads with their own bands. Reversing the invasion trend, that summer I left KUSF and *Metal Mania* #8 in the hands of Ian as I traveled Europe for six months or so. I saw the sights and most of my favorite bands—like Mercyful Fate! In Europe, I gradually heard more and more about America's best new band, Metallica, who had been storming San Francisco's Stone, Old Waldorf, and Mab clubs. When I returned, I was amazed by Metallica and the huge metal movement exploding around the Bay Area. Lars announced he was through with L.A. posers, and he and the band moved up to the East Bay. Most astonishing to me was my old buddy Pavel Baloff "singing" with a band called Exodus! Their manager Mark Whitaker let Lars Ulrich, James Hetfield, and Dave Mustaine move into his tiny house in El Cerrito.

In the last couple days of 1982, Brian Lew and I and a few select friends went to the El Cerrito house to see Metallica jam in the living room with their new bassist, Cliff. That house at 3132 Carlson Blvd. quickly turned into a party pad, the center of our world for the next few years. Rich "Banger" Burch lived just a mile to the north. The BART train, Burger King, and all-important liquor stores were just around the corner. Metallica's practice sessions in their living room were usually Smirnoff-fueled noise-athons that descended into headbanging contests or shouting melees. Metallica's poor, suffering neighbors!

Just a few miles to the south on San Pablo Avenue in Berkeley, Ruthie's Inn soon began to regularly book metal bands after being predominantly a soul and occasionally a punk venue. Ruthie's arrived just as the Berkeley Square, Keystone Berkeley, and other clubs got more uptight, leaving fewer options for rockin' bands in the East Bay. Back in the city, *Metal Mania* invited Paul, guitarists Kirk Hammett and Gary Holt, and the thundering horde of Exodus to play a benefit gig for the mag at the Mabuhay Gardens. The band "invited" some drunks onto the stage—James, Lars, and Dave—and they quickly demolished Exodus's set! Some of the crowd followed, and the barrier between *us* (metal fans) and *them* (musicians) began to crumble. That rise onto the stage had been a huge barrier, with worshippers always kept separate from their gods. The guitarist was *king*, and shredders were worshipped by crowds and their fellow musicians. At the time, Shrapnel Records owner Mike Varney successfully promoted his guitar-dominated bands and local compilation LPs like the *U.S. Metal* series throughout the world. Varney promoted many "Guitar Grudge Match" contests among our local guitar gunslingers, and they were very popular. Toward the drunken end of each of our *Metal Mania* benefits, Ian Kallen would set up a "Guitar Godathon; these were much less competitive events, which were way more about having fun.

Bay Area metal was *fun*, and becoming ever more accessible to everyone. Musicians and fans hung out together more than ever, and starting a band seemed less daunting and more exciting. The Mab being across the street from the Stone heightened this energy. Weekend nights on Broadway were usually crowded with tourists and sailors to begin with, but the introduction of often-simultaneous metal gigs soon filled the area with crazed, drunken, hooting and hollering headbangers running back and forth and around to other nearby bars and liquor stores. Broadway became a playground, and a metal mecca!

The spring of 1983 was a pivotal point, as fast-talking New Jerseyite Johnny Z. convinced Metallica to drive east in April and record their debut album out there. Before they left, Metallica headlined two stunning Stone shows, showing off their astounding new bass player, Mr. Cliff Burton. They recorded their third demo, nicknamed "The KUSF Demo" for its nearly daily presence on the station's airwaves. After the Metallic ones stole manager extraordinaire Mark Whitaker, Exodus pestered me into managing them. For one entire month, I "managed" Exodus—the only band I've ever tried that with, as I quickly learned my lesson (in violence!) and drove away two-fifths of their musicians! I could not even begin to corral the crazed Paul Baloff or the rabid Gary Holt long enough to set up meaningful gigs. Truthfully, they had wanted to get rid of

Cliff Burton's first Metallica rehearsal, December 28, 1982. Ian Kallen, Ron Quintana, James Hetfield, Lars Ulrich, Rich Pelletier BRIAN LEW

bassist Jeff Andrews for a while, but of course they had no inkling their second guitarist Kirk Hammett would take off for New York to replace Dave Mustaine in Metallica. No one in the world had suspicions about that cataclysmic event except James, Lars, and possibly Cliff.

With Adam Segan managing them, however, Exodus became kings of the Bay Area metal scene within months. Gary, Paul, and drummer Tom Hunting began writing speedier and "hella heavier" songs with their new guitarist and bassist. Exodus played every week, and got exposure everywhere around the Bay. Just like when the Ramones finally played England on July 4, 1976, and inspired nearly every punter in the audience to start up their own punk band, now every Bay Area kid who saw Exodus or Metallica seemed to be starting his own metal band.

Metal bands could play at the Stone and the two Keystone clubs on weekends, and at Ruthie's Inn all week long. The Old Waldorf moved its operations over to Wolfgang's and carried on as usual. The Mab launched regular "Brutal Sundays" plus other showcases of metal bands, and soon opened its huge upstairs Rock on Broadway club. At KUSF, the flood of local demos grew to an unstoppable deluge! Classy new bands were forming every day and thrashing all around. Out of the South Bay came Death Angel, five young cousins with an excellent pounding drummer, Andy Galeon, all of twelve years old. The city spawned molten Mordred, Maiden-ish Brocas Helm, screaming Stone Vengeance, and the hardest-rocking Anvil Chorus—who soon dominated SFHM. Even scorching metallic punks D.R.I. saw the light and emigrated from Texas to friendly San Francisco.

Increasingly, most of the new thrash brigade came out of the wild, wild East Bay. "Thrashing to the sound" and obeying Exodus's "Metal Command," musical maniacs burst out of the eastern wilderness and formed endless barbaric bands set on overrunning the civilized world. The invasion had begun earlier with Blind Illusion, Blizzard, Laaz Rockit, Hexx, Heathen, and others, but now took on a decidedly darker tint with faster, more forceful, and wicked groups like Legacy, Possessed, Attitude Adjustment, Forbidden Evil, and Vio-lence. The fastest, loudest, most underground groups were drawn to Ruthie's Inn. There the crowds grew wilder and more out of control. Especially Exodus's minions, the so-called Slay Team, Andy "Airborne" Anderson, Toby Rage, and many refugees from the dwindling punk scene, continued their crowd-walking, body-surfing, and stage-diving antics within the newly exploding thrash scene. Where it was all headbanging and fist waving in 1982, the new metal fans got more mobile, organizing impromptu mosh pits and slam dancing, as at earlier hardcore punk shows. The crossover had begun.

Ruthie's was the most fun place to hang out, as audience and performers usually got along so well. Owner Wes Robinson let us get away with almost anything, and Ruthie's became *the place* to party. You could be at the back bar of Ruthie's Inn drinking one minute, then skating across the inevitably wet ballroom floor the next, landing right in front of the band playing onstage, all in one fluid motion! Of course, more often you could be right in front of the stage enjoying some awesome musicianship before being flung by some moshing thrashers and then sliding across the floor, down the hall, and halfway out of the club, all in one shorter fluid motion.

Soon Slayer, Megadeth, Suicidal Tendencies, the Mentors, and a whole slew of L.A. thrash bands started calling Ruthie's Inn their second home. The Bay Area was a relief to these underground groups from the south. Suicidal Tendencies couldn't even play around Southern California, as they were too associated with gang culture—promoters thought too many people got shot at any show they tried to do in Los Angeles. Meanwhile, the Mentors slogged away playing for small, even hostile, crowds in the vast Hollywood clubs, but they were beloved up north. El Duce was a superstar in San Francisco. He would go from gig to bike messenger party to strip joint to almost any club and be treated like a king. Not many radio stations could play "Woman from Sodom," "Golden Showers," "The Four F Club," and other porn rock swear-fests, but Rampage Radio spun Mentors ditties almost every single week!

Ever since leaving Metallica, Dave Mustaine had threatened to bring his Fallen Angels up north to re-conquer the Bay Area and eventually the world. When Dave's new band Megadeth finally arrived, it was quite impressive—both with and without Kerry King—and we all cheered him on after the band's many early shows. From the start, Slayer's music was intense, and they seemed to adopt the rough NorCal bangers almost as much as Metallica had done. Slayer seemed to play almost every month at Ruthie's Inn or the Stone with their new buddies Exodus and Possessed. The satanic high schoolers Possessed were managed by everyone's awesome surrogate mom Debbie Abono, who fell into representing the band because guitarist Larry LaLonde was her daughter's boyfriend, and the group needed a show. Abono had so much fun handling those extreme characters that she went on to manage Forbidden, Vio-lence, Exodus, and many other groups in the close-knit family of the Bay Area metal scene.

Eventually, the scene's growth around the Bay Area led to more bands and then cool venues like the Farm or the Omni, but ultimately the local scene was totally outstripped by the explosion of popularity of heavy metal around the world. Metallica became superstars, *Headbangers Ball* ruled MTV, and record companies rushed in to sign any band with long hair. The music scene has changed tremendously in the years since, but Bay Area metal is still influential today, as evidenced by the staying power of groups like Machine Head, Autopsy, Testament, and others. Remember that while most music of the '80s and '90s totally sucked . . . BAY AREA METAL ALWAYS RULED!!!

The images in this totally amazing book are brought to you by two remarkable photographers who have lived and breathed Bay Area metal for decades. Brian Lew is a dedicated music lover, always up for a discussion about metal, grunge, or even '70s pop culture. Brian's *Whiplash* magazine was a highlight of the early metal scene—boy, was I jealous of its professional look, layout, photos, and sanctioned Mercyful Fate lyrics! The prolific Harald Oimoen is a truly gifted comedian, a king of puns and one-liners. Harald has been one of the true characters in the Bay Area scene since the beginning, and he is one of the very few people on earth who can out-talk Lars Ulrich!

Overleaf: *Beer drinkers and hell-raisers Mustaine and Hetfield backstage at the Old Waldorf, November 29, 1982, the night Metallica recorded the* Metal Up Your Ass *live demo tape.* BRIAN LEW

Facing page: *Metallica at a diner next door to the Stone before playing their first SF show, September 18, 1982.* BRIAN LEW.

This page: *Metallica back at the hotel after their first SF show, September 18, 1982.* BRIAN LEW.

James Hetfield, Ron McGovney, and Dave Mustaine load into the Old Waldorf, October 18, 1982. BRIAN LEW

From top: *Sound check, the Old Waldorf, October 18, 1982. Metallica's second visit to San Francisco.* BRIAN LEW; *James Hetfield onstage, the Old Waldorf, October 18, 1982.* BRIAN LEW

From top: *Ron McGovney and James Hetfield, the Old Waldorf, October 18, 1982.* BRIAN LEW; *McGovney and Mustaine load into the Old Waldorf, October 18, 1982.* BRIAN LEW

Facing page, from top: *Dave Mustaine, the Old Waldorf,
October 18, 1982.* BRIAN LEW; *James Hetfield, Mabuhay
Gardens, SF, November 30, 1982.* BRIAN LEW.

This page from top: *Mustaine and Hetfield,* Metal Mania
*benefit, Mabuhay Gardens, November 30, 1982. This was
Ron McGovney's last show with Metallica.* BRIAN LEW; *Lars
Ulrich, Mabuhay Gardens, November 30, 1982.* BRIAN LEW

Previous overleaf, this page, and facing page: *Garage Days Pre-visited! Metallica Mansion garage, just before Cliff's first rehearsal, December 28, 1982. These are the first photos of Cliff Burton as a member of Metallica. The garage is where the band jammed and worked on the songs that would make up* Kill 'Em All, Ride the Lightning, *and* Master of Puppets. BRIAN LEW

This page, facing page, and overleaf: *Cliff Burton's first rehearsal with Metallica, living room of the house that later became the "Metallica Mansion," December 28, 1982. There were six of us invited to attend. The furniture had been moved out of the front room or pushed to the side. During the rehearsal I sat on the couch behind Lars as he played drums. This is the same room where the band photo on the couch in* Master of Puppets *was taken.* BRIAN LEW

James Hetfield, the Stone, March 5, 1983. BRIAN LEW

THE STONE AND THE KEYSTONES

METALLICA, THE STONE, MARCH 5, 1983

by Brian Lew, excerpt from Metal Mania #10, 1983

Six months have passed since METALLICA's dubious San Francisco debut opening for BITCH in September of '82, but in those two hundred-odd days the group has built up a large, rabid following in the Bay Area. This particular show was dubbed "The Night Of The Banging Head" and was the debut of new bassist, Cliff Burton. As a crowd of three hundred or so filed into The Stone, the scene was set for what turned out to be the heaviest show in recent S.F. HM history!

Opening the show were LAAZ ROCKIT and EXODUS. The awesome EXODUS bludgeoned the bangers into submission and induced some wild thrashing on the dance floor with such murderous tunes as "Whipping Queen," "Die By His Hand," and "Impaler." Despite an ecstatic crowd response, EXODUS were denied an encore, but they nonetheless wreaked havoc on craniums and left many a sore neck!

On the other hand, East Bay PRIEST/CRUE clones LAAZ ROCKIT were criminally lacking in originality. Although they do have a good stage presence and show, utilizing some effective lighting, and their new guitarist definitely improves them as a performing unit, their weak, predictable material overshadows these good points. At last, LAAZ completed their alloted set and were gone. Then it was time...

METALLICA, those Supreme Metal Gods, those Purveyers of Raging Sonic Decapitation, those Rabid Vodka-Powered Maniacs, blew our faces off as they stormed onstage through a flurry of smoke and blinding light and got things really banging with "Hit The Lights" and it was time to DIE!!!

As is their style, the band went from power to power as they steamed through "The Mechanix" and "Phantom Lord", leaving the headbanging horde thrashed and raging, and it was only three songs into the set! The autobiographical "Motorbreath" was as fast as ever and even more plaster cascaded from the ceiling. At this show, the group was incorporating some new lighting and effects and the results were staggering! Their live show is now complete and is the most effective of any club band I've seen!

Next up was the fiery cauldron of "Jump In The Fire" and then that "war machine that eats its way across the land," "No Remorse"! DEATH, DEATH, RESOUNDING DEATH!!! And still METALLICA mercilessly hacked through their list of nuclear soul shatterers. "Seek And Destroy" found its target and drilled our eardrums as the headbanging and thrashing of the crowd (and band) intensified.

The moment many had been waiting for soon arrived. Bassist Cliff Burton's solo spot!!! Cliff built his solo from a haunting classical guitar-sounding ballad up to a crescendo of some of the fastest, most apocalyptic bass raging ever performed! Step aside Steve Harris, Bill Sheehan and Joey DeMaio!

Throughout his symphony, Cliff (a.k.a. God!) utilized his wah pedal to attain sunds that most would believe impossible; you could swear he was playing lead guitar, not bass. As his solo built up to its conclusion, drummer supreme Lars Ulrich (now playing double bass) and maestro of the six string Dave Mustaine leaped into an awesome jam session that had heads bobbing violently and hair flying in all directions. Then, in one swift action, they were rejoined by vocalist/rhythm guitarist/rager James Hetfield and sped into that ear bleeding anthem "Whiplash."

As the crowd "banged their heads against the stage like they never did before," the group continued to go mental right along with them! Closing the set were the two DIAMOND HEAD classics "Am I Evil?" and "The Prince," which were played, in traditional METALLICA fashion, faster than Sean Harris, et al, could ever dream possible!

For their well-deserved (and loudly requested) encores, METALLICA brought back a song they performed in their early days, BLITZKRIEG's bombastic "Blitzkreig" (Raging Metallic Death!!!) and then obliterated everyone and everything as they sliced into that anthem to end all anthems, the almighty ode to headbangers "Metal Militia"!!

With the addition of Cliff Burton, METALLICA now have the heaviest and fastest lineup ever assembled. With dates confirmed for them in New York in early April (including a headlining show on the 1st and a support slot with VANDENBERG on the 8th), and their debut album expected in late spring, things are definitely beginning to happen for this band!

Above: *Preparing for sound check before Cliff's first show, the Stone, March 5, 1983. Cliff is on the far left and Lars is behind the drums. This is when Metallica only needed a wooden ladder to set up their show.* BRIAN LEW. Right: *Cliff during his first sound check with Metallica, March 5, 1983.* BRIAN LEW

Above and overleaf: *Metallica's first sound check with new bassist Cliff Burton, March 5, 1983.* BRIAN LEW

Above, left, and following pages: *Metallica's*
as a hometown San Francisco band, also first t
onstage with Cliff Burton, the Stone, March 5,
Note explosion of Metallica logos. BRIAN LEW

Facing page: *Cliff Burton performing his first bass solo with Metallica, the Stone, March 5, 1983.* BRIAN LEW

Facing page, bottom: *Preshow video interview, the Stone, March 5, 1983.* BRIAN LEW

Facing page and above: *Cliff's second show with Metallica, also Dave Mustaine's last SF show with the band, the Stone, March 19, 1983.* BRIAN LEW

From top: *Paul Baloff of Exodus, Mabuhay Gardens, May 15, 1983.*
BRIAN LEW; *Kirk Hammett of Exodus, the Stone, March 5, 1983,*
opening for Metallica at Cliff's first show. BRIAN LEW

Exodus after Kirk Hammett. Clockwise from top: Mike Maung, Rob McKillop, and Gary Holt, the Old Waldorf, 1983. BRIAN LEW; *Exodus with new guitarist Rick Hunolt (and manager Adam Segan), Wolfgang's, SF, January 30, 1984.* BRIAN LEW; *Gary Holt with short-term replacement Evan McCaskey, Keystone Berkeley, 1983.* BRIAN LEW

73

From top: Metallica, *Keystone Palo Alto, Halloween 1983.* HARALD OIMOEN; *James Hetfield and underwater Cliff Burton, Keystone Palo Alto, September 1, 1983* HARALD OIMOEN. Facing page: *Keystone Palo Alto, Halloween 1983.* HARALD OIMOEN. Overleaf: *Keystone Palo Alto, September 1, 1983. This was the first time I ever saw Metallica. I was blown away by their fierce, in-yer-face live show.* HARALD OIMOEN

Facing page: *James Hetfield, Keystone Palo Alto, Halloween 1983. James later confessed to me that this guitar wasn't a real Gibson. He put a Gibson nameplate on it, because he didn't want anyone to know he was playing a cheap imitation copy.* HARALD OIMOEN.

Above and next two pages: *Keystone Palo Alto, Halloween 1983.* HARALD OIMOEN

Clockwise from top: *My best-known shot, from the back of* Ride the Lightning. *Cliff told me he dug this shot because he was doing a sick string-bend. Unfortunately, this signed duplicate is the only one in existence, since I never got the original negative back from Cliff.* HARALD OIMOEN; *Cliff's second choice for the back of* Ride the Lightning, *which I personally think is far superior, also from a signed negative.* HARALD OIMOEN; *Cliff Burton headbanging at half-speed, Keystone Palo Alto, Halloween 1983.* HARALD OIMOEN. *Facing page: Cliff Burton, Keystone Palo Alto, Halloween 1983.* HARALD OIMOEN

Above: *Cliff and James, Keystone Palo Alto, Halloween 1983.* BRIAN LEW.

Facing page, clockwise from top left: *Keystone Palo Alto, Halloween 1983.* BRIAN LEW; *Keystone Palo Alto, Halloween 1983.* HARALD OIMOEN; *Keystone Palo Alto,*

Above, clockwise from top: *Keystone Palo Alto, Halloween 1983.* BRIAN LEW. *Keystone Palo Alto, Halloween 1983.* HARALD OIMOEN; *Keystone Palo Alto,*

Halloween 1983. BRIAN LEW. Facing page: *Cliff Burton, Keystone Palo Alto, Halloween 1983.* BRIAN LEW

Rich "Bang That Head That Doesn't Bang" Burch onstage with Metallica, Keystone Palo Alto, Halloween 1983. BRIAN LEW

Cliff brings the hammer down on Lars, Keystone Palo Alto, Halloween 1983. BRIAN LEW

Facing page and this page: *Metallica, the Stone, November 26, 1983. The stage was much lower and the crowds were more violent at the Stone than at the Keystone Palo Alto, so I invested in a zoom lens to better capture the action and keep a safe distance.* HARALD OIMOEN

Facing page: *Slayer, the Stone, May 24, 1984.* HARALD OIMOEN.

Above: *First Slayer show in SF, Wolfgang's, January 30, 1984. After playing the Keystone Berkeley three days earlier, Slayer took off their makeup and kept it off.* BRIAN LEW

Slayer arrives at the Stone and finds a home in SF, 1984. This page, clockwise from top left: *Dave Lombardo.* HARALD OIMOEN; *Kerry King.* HARALD OIMOEN; *Jeff Hanneman.* HARALD OIMOEN. Facing page, clockwise from left: *Tom Araya drinking for four, backstage at the Stone.* HARALD OIMOEN; *Slayer guitarists in the Stone dressing room.* HARALD OIMOEN; *Jeff Hanneman in a black-magic moment.* HARALD OIMOEN

Facing page from top: *Megadeth sound check with Kerry King in the band, Ruthie's Inn, February 17, 1984.* BRIAN LEW. *Megadeth's second show, Ruthie's Inn, February 17, 1984.* BRIAN LEW. Above: *Megadeth with second guitarist Kerry King, Keystone Palo Alto, April 16, 1984.* HARALD OIMOEN. Overleaf: *Megadeth, Keystone Palo Alto, April 16, 1984. Note former Metallica bassist Ron McGovney in the crowd and young Brian Lew down front with his trusty camera around his neck. Toby Rage seems to be tearing is hair out with frustration, probably because the crowd seems too small to break his fall when stagediving.* HARALD OIMOEN.

Above: *Megadeth sound-check at the Keystone Berkeley, April 15, 1984.* BRIAN LEW.

Facing page: *Dave Mustaine in Megadeth, Keystone Palo Alto, April 16, 1984.* HARALD OIMOEN

Facing and this page: *"Paid assassin" Kerry King wearing a Satanic wrestling belt and Dave Mustaine wearing a grenade in Megadeth, Keystone Palo Alto, April 16, 1984.* HARALD OIMOEN

Clockwise from upper left: *Dave Mustaine and hand grenades onstage at Ruthie's Inn during Megadeth's second show, February 17, 1984.* BRIAN LEW; *Dave Mustaine during sound check, Ruthie's Inn, February 17, 1984.* BRIAN LEW; *Kerry King during Megadeth sound check, Keystone Berkeley, April 15, 1984.* BRIAN LEW

This page: Dave Mustaine, the Stone, 1984. Above: Dave
demonstrates a difficult guitar-god backbend move. HARALD OIMOEN

From top: *Megadeth and Exodus at the Stone, 1984. "Mexodus" or "Exodeth"?* HARALD OIMOEN; *Megadeth three-piece lineup on the sidewalk outside the Stone, 1984.* HARALD OIMOEN; *A short-lived Megadeth lineup including ex–Captain Beefheart guitarist Mike Albert (far right).* HARALD OIMOEN

Mustaine with his two favorite girls, his B.C. Rich Bich guitars, his weapons of choice in Metallica and early Megadeth.

Facing page: *Megadeth, Ruthie's Inn, February 17, 1984. The infamous Mustaine sneer was more extreme and obvious after his lips were shocked several times that night by an ungrounded microphone.* HARALD OIMOEN. Above: *"Hello, me, it's me again . . ." Dave Mustaine, the Stone. Dave was a total trip, pissed off at the world. He was always more into doing photos when he was drunk or stoned.* HARALD OIMOEN.

Overleaf: *Megadeth in front of the Stone in SF's North Beach with onetime manager Peter Schnell and "Airborne" Andy Anderson. The Mabuhay Gardens and the Rock on Broadway are across the street.* HARALD OIMOEN

Anthrax, Fistful of Metal *tour, the
Kabuki, July 7, 1984. Anthrax's first SF
show was classic. Exodus opened and
just crushed them completely. They were
completely out of their element here!*
HARALD OIMOEN

From top: *Metal pen pals Alan Blagrave, Corinne Lynn, and Gerald Yoshida from Canada make a pilgrimage to the Bay Area, 1983.* BRIAN LEW. *Lars Ulrich executes a Men at Work album in front of the Record Vault at its first location, 1920 Polk Street, SF, September 3, 1983.* WAYNE VANDERKUIL. *Overleaf: Execution of Men at Work album complete!* WAYNE VANDERKUIL

From top: *Cliff Burton signs a deadly autograph for John Scharpen at the Record Vault, September 3, 1983.* WAYNE VANDERKUIL; *Motörhead's Lemmy Kilmister with owners Zary and Pam, the Record Vault, later 2423 Polk Street location, October 1986.* TIM HEALY. Facing page from top: *James sinks his teeth into the remains of a Men at Work album, the Record Vault, September 3, 1983.* WAYNE VANDERKUIL; *Lars and James signing vinyl and denim jackets at the Record Vault before the final show of the Kill 'Em All for One tour with Raven, September 3, 1983.* WAYNE VANDERKUIL

From top: *Metal madness as Metallica attempts to play a secret show, Mabuhay Gardens, July 20, 1984.* BRIAN LEW; *Metallica stopped home after spending most of 1984 in Europe recording* Ride the Lightning *and playing the Seven Dates of Hell tour. They set up an SF gig incognito as "the Four Horsemen"—the club door actually billed them as "Kill 'Em All." Either way, this was the worst-kept secret imaginable; mobs of people were turned away. Then the club had to position a wall of security dudes in front of the stage to hold everybody back. That didn't stop Toby Rage from pouring a huge pitcher of beer on James Hetfield's head.* HARALD OIMOEN. Facing page: *Metallica secret show, Mabuhay Gardens, July 20, 1984.* HARALD OIMOEN

Clockwise from top left: *Cliff Burton demonic, Metallica secret show, Mabuhay Gardens, July 20, 1984.* HARALD OIMOEN; *Cliff ecstatic, laughing at a fearless photographer who had scaled the lighting rig, Mabuhay Gardens, July 20, 1984.* HARALD OIMOEN; *Kirk and Cliff (and James's middle finger) review Ron Quintana's Metal Mania.* HARALD OIMOEN

Exodus Bonded by Blood back cover shots.

HARALD OIMOEN, GODDAMMIT!

Above: *Exodus in Davis Park, San Pablo, 1983. Photo session for* Whiplash *fanzine.* BRIAN LEW. Facing page, clockwise from top:

Exodus, Day in the Dirt, Aquatic Park, Berkeley, August 19, 1984. BRIAN LEW; *Gary Holt, Aquatic Park, August 19, 1984.* BRIAN LEW;

Toby Rage onstage with Exodus adding "Slay Team" vocals, Aquatic Park, August 19, 1984. BRIAN LEW.

This page and following pages: *Slayer, Aquatic Park, August 19, 1984.* HARALD OIMOEN

Slayer's Dave Lombardo, Aquatic Park, August 19, 1984. HARALD OIMOEN

Slayer at dusk, Aquatic Park, August 19, 1984. BRIAN LEW

Slayer's Kerry King, Aquatic Park, August 19, 1984. HARALD OIMOEN

Above: Toby Rage practices walking on heads. HARALD OIMOEN

Above and facing page: *This series of shots with members of Slayer, Exodus, Possessed, and Suicidal Tendencies happened naturally, with a few people getting together for a photo and calling over to their pals. Before I knew it a mob had congregated, and I just started snapping away frantically. Then Toby Rage came running at a breakneck pace and proceeded to hit Doug Goodman square in the jaw.* HARALD OIMOEN

Jeff Hanneman of Slayer, Jeff Becerra of Possessed, and Tom Hunting of Exodus hanging out at Slayer's van, Aquatic Park, August 19, 1984. HARALD OIMOEN

From top: *Slayer mobbing Tom Araya, who is dressed like a follower of Suicidal Tendencies in flannel shirt and headband. Suicidal played almost completely* *that day, with security guards shining flashlights on the bass and guitar.* HARALD OIMOEN; *Tom Araya, Aquatic Park, August 19, 1984.* HARALD OIMOEN

From top: *Slayer and Exodus, Day in the Dirt, August 19, 1984. These bands totally dug each other's music. They competed in a friendly way to outdo each other in heaviness, always keeping tabs on each other's material.* ; *New wave Kerry King, Aquatic Park, August 19, 1984.*

From top: *Strange as it seems, in the beginning Legacy wore priest collars in an attempt to define a band image. The lineup at this early show is, from left to right: Eric Peterson, Louie Clemente, Steve "Zetro" Souza, Greg Christian, and Eric's cousin Derrick Ramirez.* HARALD OIMOEN; *Eric Peterson of Legacy.* HARALD OIMOEN

Toby Rage walking on heads at a Death Angel show, Mabuhay Gardens. Along with "Airborne" Andy Anderson and a few others, Toby was a part of Exodus's crew, the "Slay Team," who set new standards in stage-diving. If a crowd was packed tightly enough, he would jump onto the crowd and walk on the heads, necks, and shoulders of unsuspecting punters, usually zooming halfway across the club before sinking back into the mosh pit. What a sight to behold! We would dare Toby to jump off the highest PA stacks, which he did without hesitation or any signs of fear of injury or bodily harm. HARALD OIMOEN

From top: *Dave Mustaine with Aerosmith's Brad Whitford. Aerosmith had a night off in SF, and Whitford and drummer Joey Kramer decided to check out a Megadeth show. Mustaine was visibly psyched to meet one of his idols.* HARALD OIMOEN; *Gary Holt and Kirk Hammett, two of the most influential lead guitarists in thrash metal. At one point they shared guitar duties in Exodus, the band Hammett started with drummer Tom Hunting.* HARALD OIMOEN

From top: *Kirk Hammett showing off his Fernandes "Edna" model. Kirk had cleverly defaced an extra Fernandes decal to spell "Edna,"*
Metallica's slang term for groupies. HARALD OIMOEN; *Bay Area guitar gods at Ruthie's Inn, left to right: Doug Piercy of Heathen/Anvil Chorus,*
Kirk Hammett, Kurdt Vanderhoof of Metal Church, Gary Holt, and Thaen Rasmussen of Anvil Chorus. HARALD OIMOEN. Overleaf: *Kerry King*
and Jeff Hanneman of Slayer, Keystone Palo Alto. HARALD OIMOEN

This page, clockwise from top: *Tom Araya, Dave Lombardo, and Jeff Hanneman of Slayer outside Ruthie's Inn.* HARALD OIMOEN;

Dave Lombardo. HARALD OIMOEN; *Jeff Hanneman and Kerry King reigning, Keystone Palo Alto.* HARALD OIMOEN

Clockwise from top: *Tom Araya and Kerry King of Slayer.* HARALD OIMOEN; *Tom Araya.* HARALD OIMOEN; *Slayer live onstage.* HARALD OIMOEN; *Kerry King.* HARALD OIMOEN

From top: *Jeff Hanneman and Kerry King in action, Keystone Palo Alto.* HARALD OIMOEN; *Another one of my most infamous (yet long uncredited) shots, Slayer live as seen on the back cover of* Hell Awaits, *Keystone Palo Alto.* HARALD FUCKING OIMOEN

This page: *Slayer live at Ruthie's Inn.*
HARALD OIMOEN. Next page: *Kerry King
live at Ruthie's Inn.* HARALD OIMOEN.
Following page: *Jeff Hanneman
executes a full backbend onstage with
Slayer, Ruthie's Inn.* HARALD OIMOEN

Previous overleaf: *Dave Lombardo of Slayer. At this time I could easily walk onto the middle of the stage and shoot Lombardo below the drum riser while the show raged around me.* HARALD OIMOEN; This page: *Slayer road trip, Starry Night, Portland, OR, August 27, 1985. The shot of Kerry King flipping me off reminds me of the classic photo of Johnny Cash giving Jim Marshall's camera a big middle finger.* HARALD OIMOEN

From top: *Kerry King, Starry Night, August 27, 1985.* HARALD OIMOEN; *Toby Rage onstage with Slayer, Starry Night, August 27, 1985. At one point, Debbie Abono, the surrogate mother of our scene, thought things were getting out of hand, so she pulled Toby aside and said: "This is the Slayer show, it isn't the Toby show!"* HARALD OIMOEN

From top: *Kerry King when he was still moonlighting on the side with Megadeth.* HARALD OIMOEN; *Slayer/municipal pool sign from Salinas.* HARALD OIMOEN. Facing page: *Kerry King's road case, 1985.* HARALD OIMOEN

From top: *Exodus, Slayer, and other heavies behind the Crest Theatre, Sacramento, April 13, 1985.* HARALD OIMOEN; *The Exodus attack—Paul Baloff takes a bite of Slayer's Jeff Hanneman.* HARALD OIMOEN; *Dave Mustaine and Exodus hit it off so well because they both loved to party heavily. On far right is Megadeth's first manager, Jay Jones.* HARALD OIMOEN

From top: *Slayer's Dave Lombardo and Exodus's Rick Hunolt and Tom Hunting, Sacramento, April 13, 1985.* HARALD OIMOEN; *Jeff Hanneman and Gary Holt (and their beers).* HARALD OIMOEN. Overleaf: *Gary Holt and Paul Baloff onstage in Exodus, Crest Theatre, April 13, 1985. Paul was an awesome front man. He went through an exercise routine onstage, just by running around like a madman.* HARALD OIMOEN

From top: *Gary Holt sashays across the Kaiser Convention Center stage, Oakland, July 26, 1985.* HARALD OIMOEN; *"Exotallica" in Petaluma, left to right:*
Kirk Hammett, Paul Baloff, Gary Holt, James Hetfield, Mark Whitaker, Rick Hunolt, and Spastik Children front man Fred "Rotten" Cotton HARALD OIMOEN

From top: John Marshall, Kirk Hammett, and the future Rebecca Hammett at the Keystone Palo Alto, Halloween 1983. The show's set list for "Clifford" taped to the wall behind them contains cues for when Cliff should talk to the crowd. BRIAN LEW; *"Exotallica" returns—the Bay Area's heaviest two bands getting drunk together at an Uli Roth Show at Wolfgang's, May 16, 1985.* HARALD OIMOEN

This page: *Exodus, Kabuki Theater, March 15, 1985.* HARALD OIMOEN

Clockwise from top: *Rick Hunolt, Kabuki Theater, March 15, 1985.* HARALD OIMOEN; *All of Rick Hunolt but one tooth.* HARALD OIMOEN;
Exodus's deadly guitar duo of Rick Hunolt and Gary Holt. HARALD OIMOEN

Facing page, above, and following pages: *Metallica and Slayer at the Kabuki Theater, April 12, 1985. I introduced the two bands backstage; they had never met. There was a weird vibe at first because they had slagged each other off so much in the press. Brian Slagel in the Slayer corner at top left on this page. Jeff Hanneman appears to be preparing to hit James over the head in the top photo on the facing page. At one point, Dave Lombardo and Lars Ulrich began comparing callouses.* HARALD OIMOEN

Above: *Lars and Kirk were obviously very inebriated but still very cooperative with my photo taking, and actually insisted that I take a bunch more shots.* HARALD OIMOEN.

Right: *Lars and Kirk bump with Possessed manager Debbie Abono.* HARALD OIMOEN.

Overleaf: *James Hetfield, the Stone, June 15, 1987. As Metallica started to finally get more popular, they were recognized at gigs a lot. Here James hides behind a big post, with his girlfriend Teresa. Look closely for Phil Demmel of Vio-lence/Machine Head and David Godfrey of Heathen hiding out in the open in the shot, too.* HARALD OIMOEN

Exodus, Ruthie's Inn, 1984. BRIAN LEW

RUTHIE'S INN

THE BIRTHPLACE OF VIOLENCE

by Gary Holt

I remember the first time we ever walked through the door of Ruthie's Inn to play a gig. It was Exodus and some random rock bands; the kind where it's them, their sisters, and family members and shit like that. They had no idea what they were getting into, but I don't think any of us realized that night what Ruthie's would eventually mean to Exodus, and to Bay Area thrash metal in general. I'll never forget taking the stage that night, and our friends and fans smashing all the drink glasses the "rock" band's friends had left on the front of the stage. Blood and broken glass were everywhere! Some girl who was with that other crowd actually seemed to enjoy our set. She was front row until Paul Baloff smeared his hand in a puddle of blood and wiped it on her face. You could hear her screaming clear as a bell over the volume! And that was only the start of something big!

The song "Bonded by Blood" is basically our ode to Ruthie's Inn. The "blood upon the stage" line is a direct reference to that moment, and also to our past propensity for becoming blood brothers with our entire inner circle, something I'd be loath to do now! It was our way of immortalizing a club in song, I guess, and no club ever deserved it more. This was the place where the pit really became what it is today; fist banging gave way to stage diving and all-around mayhem, due in large part to our crossover audience of metalheads and punks. This was where the shit truly hit the proverbial fan.

Ruthie's was the brainchild of Wes Robinson, and we were all the ill-behaved children who by some miracle never were dragged away in handcuffs. Paul and I developed this obsession with slicing the shirts of hair bands up into little badges of honor worn around our wrists. Look at old pictures of Pavel and you'll see what I mean. He was covered in 'em. Our antics have since become urban legend, the whole "someone was killed because Paul said, 'Go out and kill a poser'" thing. I don't think we could have avoided jail time for that one, but I'm still asked to this day if there's any truth to the story! Paul did have a way of mak-

ing those deemed to be "posers" nervous when he'd call for their heads, but I don't think capital murder ever occurred as a result! Things did quite often get out of hand, but we felt like we owned the place anyway. We pretty much did whatever we wanted, and we drank. A lot.

From my twenty-first birthday party, to our first show together with Slayer, to all the shows with everyone from Death Angel, Possessed, Vio-lence, Legacy, and many others, no club ever became to this band what Ruthie's was. Even though we started at places like the Old Waldorf, the Mabuhay Gardens, the Stone, Wolfgang's and many others, it's Ruthie's that lives in infamy because it's the one and only birthplace of violence becoming part and parcel of an Exodus show. I had never seen a stage dive, a pit, or anything coming close to resembling that before Ruthie's. It was born there, and anyone who says different doesn't know what they're talking about or they're lying to you. It started there, with the help of Wes Robinson and the Slay Team (Toby Rage, R.I.P. my brother). While the rest of the metal world would later come around and learn the joys of a little good friendly violent fun, it all started *there*, at Ruthie's, end of story.

A typical Ruthie's Inn mob scene, including the blatantly underage Death Angel, Debbie Abono, and Ruthie's fixture Big Daddy, at far right. One night a couple of miscellaneous cretins attempted to sneak into Ruthie's through some ventilation ducts above the main floor in the center of the club. Big Daddy was somewhat in charge of security, so when he saw some legs dangling from the ceiling he started spraying a can of mace wildly in the air at the gate jumpers! Cliff Burton happened to be standing nearby, and the mist hit him directly in the face. He completely freaked out. The first ticket dodger was apprehended and kicked out by some other security goons as soon as he came through the vent. Meanwhile, Cliff started reading "Big Dummy" the riot act, all the while wiping his burning eyes. He was right in Big Daddy's face, yelling about how irresponsible and stupid he was for spraying that crap with so many people around in such a small space. I had never seen Cliff so pissed off, ever. He was absolutely livid! Cliff demanded free drinks for him and a couple pals as some kind of compensation for such a major fuckup. Big Daddy totally apologized, kissed Cliff's ass big-time, and wisely told Irving, the bartender, to give Cliff all the drinks he wanted on the house for the rest of the evening. HARALD OIMOEN

Dogpile in front of Ruthie's Inn, left to right: Unknown banger, Debbie Abono's bright eyes, Mike Sus, unknown banger #2, unknown smoking banger, sky-high occasional Metallica guitarist John Marshall, Toby Rage, Karen Waller McDaniel, Lonnie Hunolt, Mike Torrao, Karen's pal, unknown new waver. Toby Rage is exposing himself, and I don't think Lonnie Hunolt noticed Toby's schlong in his face until after I snapped the shot! HARALD OIMOEN

A great example of how the wall between bands and fans did not exist in the Bay Area. Left to right: Dan Lara, Erik Lannon, Cliff Burton, unknown banger, Rob McKillop, Rick Strahl, Alexis Olson, Craig Behrhorst, Andy Anderson (upside down), Rick Hunolt's brother Lonnie, unknown banger, Adam Segan, unknown banger.
HARALD OIMOEN

Scenes from Gary Holt's 21st birthday party, Ruthie's Inn, May 4, 1985. Lots of photo shoots happened in the Ruthie's men's room, as random people would drift in and join the festivities. HARALD OIMOEN. Facing page, clockwise from top left: Lars Ulrich shows off a borrowed laminate he used to sneak backstage at a Laaz Rockit gig at the Stone. HARALD OIMOEN; "Hello, me, it's the other me . . ." Kirk Hammett looks through the looking glass at Ruthie's Inn. HARALD OIMOEN; James Hetfield at the back bar of Ruthie's Inn. HARALD OIMOEN. Overleaf: Exodus gets another bright idea. Gary Holt's mom's garage, El Sobrante. HARALD OIMOEN.

Facing page: *Paul Baloff, Wolfgang's, July 11, 1983.* BRIAN LEW. This page: *Exodus, Ruthie's Inn, 1984.* BRIAN LEW

From top: *Exodus, Wolfgang's, January 30, 1984.* BRIAN LEW; *Exodus crowd action, Wolfgang's, January 30, 1984.* BRIAN LEW

Top left and right: *Exodus supporting Loudness, Wolfgang's, July 11, 1983.* BRIAN LEW.

Bottom: *Exodus and Slayer backstage at Wolfgang's, January 30, 1984.* BRIAN LEW

Exodus, Wolfgang's, January 30, 1984. BRIAN LEW

Paul Baloff of Exodus, Petaluma. Feeling the power of a wall of sonic sound, with amps turned up to ten! HARALD OIMOEN

From top: *Kerry King behind Ruthie's Inn.* HARALD OIMOEN; *Slayer backstage at Ruthie's Inn.* HARALD OIMOEN

From top: *Dave Lombardo and Tom Araya of Slayer.* HARALD OIMOEN; *Jeff Hanneman of Slayer. Before I had a flash on my camera, I had to ask everyone to stand directly underneath a*

Facing page: Jeff Hanneman the can man. HARALD OIMOEN. *This page, from top: Kerry King plays bartender.*
HARALD OIMOEN; *Dave Lombardo, Teresa Lombardo, and Jeff Hanneman fly the flannel, Salinas.* HARALD OIMOEN

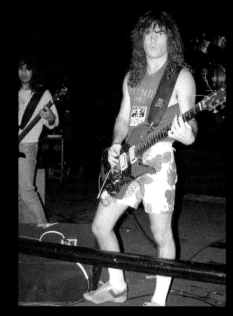

Slayer's brutal onstage live shows contrasted heavily with their easygoing offstage demeanor (not to mention their wardrobe!). HARALD OIMOEN

Early shots of Forbidden Evil, before they dropped the "Evil" and became Forbidden, featuring future Vio-lence guitarist/Machine Head front man Robb Flynn and future Slayer drummer Paul Bostaph. HARALD OIMOEN

Facing page, from top: *Legacy's first photo shoot, with backdrop and drumheads by Metallica designer Mark DeVito.* HARALD OIMOEN;
Ruthie's fixture Legacy onstage, Ruthie's Inn. HARALD OIMOEN. This page, from top: *Legacy backstage at Ruthie's Inn, shortly before the
band became Testament. With its colorful graffiti, this tiny room made an ideal setting for many thrasher group shots.* HARALD OIMOEN; *Mike
"Yaz" Jastremski of Griffin/Heathen, one of Cliff Burton's best pals, with Alex Skolnick and Eric Peterson, Ruthie's Inn.* HARALD OIMOEN

From top: *Mark Osegueda and Rob Cavestany of Death Angel, Ruthie's Inn.* HARALD OIMOEN; *Death Angel drummer Andy Galeon and Dave Mustaine, the Stone. The little drummer boy was all of 12 years old when he helped his cousins form the band.* HARALD OIMOEN.
Facing page: *Jeff Becerra of Possessed,* Seven Churches *photo shoot, manager Debbie Abono's backyard, Pinole.* HARALD OIMOEN

Possessed, Seven Churches *photo shoot. Clockwise from top left: Jeff Becerra, Mike Sus, Mike Torrao preparing to drink from the goble of gore, Torrao drinking it down. The fog machine was made by Debbie's son Rick out of a pickle barrel and a hair dryer, and it worked ncredibly well.* HARALD OIMOEN. *Facing page: Possessed, Seven Churches photo shoot.* HARALD OIMOEN.

Possessed, Seven Churches *photo shoot. At the time, most Bay Area bangers didn't take Possessed seriously. They were considered Slayer clones who ripped their image off from Kerry King and company. But when I traveled to Seattle and Portland with them in 1985, they were treated like gods and given incredible responses. They are true death metal originators.* HARALD OIMOEN. Facing page, from top: *Larry LaLonde seeks his next victim.* HARALD OIMOEN; *Mike Torrao takes an axe to Toby Rage. Ketchup and red food coloring–laced corn syrup abound.* HARALD OIMOEN. Overleaf: *Death metal guitar god Larry LaLonde (with Toby Rage hidden behind the Marshalls holding Larry's legs in place).* HARALD OIMOEN

From top: *This could be the exact moment crossover was born: Dave Lombardo in the front row of a D.R.I. show. He already knew all the words.* HARALD OIMOEN; *Punk and metal worlds collide in a blur: drummers Felix Griffin of D.R.I. and Dave Lombardo of Slayer.* HARALD OIMOEN

Suicidal Tendencies, New Varsity Theater, Palo Alto, October 11, 1985. Suicidal was the first punk band I liked, and their pits were always super-violent. Clockwise from top: *This random punk stage-diver is Chris Kontos. He cut his Mohawk and later played drums in Machine Head, Verbal Abuse, Exodus, Death Angel, Testament, and Attitude Adjustment, among others.* HARALD OIMOEN; *Rocky George and Mike Muir onstage.* HARALD OIMOEN; *Mike Muir of Suicidal Tendencies.* HARALD OIMOEN

Clockwise from top left: *Spike Cassidy of
D.R.I., my current bandmate and partner
in crime.* HARALD OIMOEN; *Jello Biafra, one
of the last Dead Kennedys shows, the
Stone, February 16, 1986.* HARALD OIMOEN;
*Poison Idea front man Jerry A., the Stone,
May 15, 1988.* HARALD OIMOEN

Clockwise from top: *One of my favorite shots of the always bizarre and hilarious El Duce.* HARALD OIMOEN; *The Mentors—unmasked!—in all of their unhooded glory with Ruthie's Inn promoter Wes Robinson. Left to right: El Duce (Eldon Hoke), Dr. Heathen Scum (Steve Broy), Sickie Wifebeater (Eric Carlson), and Robinson.* HARALD OIMOEN; *Doochie living the high life.* HARALD OIMOEN

*Possessed, Ruthie's Inn. I always wondered how this
guy achieved such a strange airborne trajectory.*
HARALD OIMOEN

Facing page from top: *Possessed onstage, Ruthie's Inn. The closest Ruthie's ever came to having stage effects—probably the same pickle-barrel/hair-dryer fog machine we used for the album cover.* HARALD OIMOEN; *Jeff Becerra and Mike Torrao of Possessed, Ruthie's Inn. Becerra is wearing a Sammy Hagar shirt turned inside out—the ultimate evil!* HARALD OIMOEN. This page: *Possessed onstage, reigning in full Satanic metal regalia, Ruthie's Inn.* HARALD OIMOEN

From top: *Possessed onstage, Ruthie's Inn. Truth be told, guitarist Larry LaLonde was never comfortable with the band's evil Satanic image, and quickly adopted standard Motörhead-shirt-and-jeans metalhead attire.* HARALD OIMOEN; *LaLonde at an earlier gig, resplendent in formal full Satanic metal regalia.* HARALD OIMOEN

Clockwise from top: *Possessed after a triumphant gig opening for Slayer on the Live Undead mini-tour, Starry Night, August 27, 1985.* HARALD OIMOEN; *Possessed manager Debbie Abono, the nicest, friendliest lady anyone could ever meet, loved by everyone in the scene. When it came down to business, though, she was tough as nails and didn't take any shit from anyone.* HARALD OIMOEN; *Pre-gig Possessed in less Satanic typical teenager T-shirts*

Clockwise from top: *Exodus and Possessed dogpile, featuring, from left to right: Paul Baloff, Mike Sus (top), Toby Rage, Paul Baloff's girlfriend Lizzie, Peter Carter (top), Larry LaLonde (top), Legacy manager Alexis Olsen (lying across), an unknown headbanger, Gary Holt's buried head, Tom Hunting (top), Andy Anderson, Rick Hunolt, Donnie Griggs (top), Mike Torrao, and a second unknown banger.* HARALD OIMOEN; *James Hetfield and two rookies share cans of something strangely nonalcoholic.* HARALD OIMOEN; *Possessed's Mike Sus and Mike Torrao.* HARALD OIMOEN

Above from left: Fred "Rotten" Cotton in full-on Spastik Children mode with James Hetfield modeling homemade Spastik shirt. HARALD OIMOEN; Spastik Children's incredible drummer Jimmy Hatfield, using a hubcap as a cymbal and two kitchen chairs as a drum stool. HARALD OIMOEN. Below: Best known for the hit "The Ballad of Harald O.," the class-sick Spastik Children lineup, left to right: James "Flunky" McDaniel, Clifford Burton, Fred "Rotten" Cotton, and Jaymz "Bobby Brady" Hetfield. HARALD OIMOEN

Facing page: *The Infamous Metallica Mansion where James and Lars lived for many years, 3132 Carlson Blvd., El Cerrito.* HARALD OIMOEN: *James Hetfield relaxing at the Metallica Mansion. I admit being disappointed during my first visit that the house was not actually a mansion.* HARALD OIMOEN. *This page and following page: A typical spur-of-the-moment photo on at home with the two main Metalli-fuckers Lars Ulrich and James Hetfield.* HARALD OIMOEN.

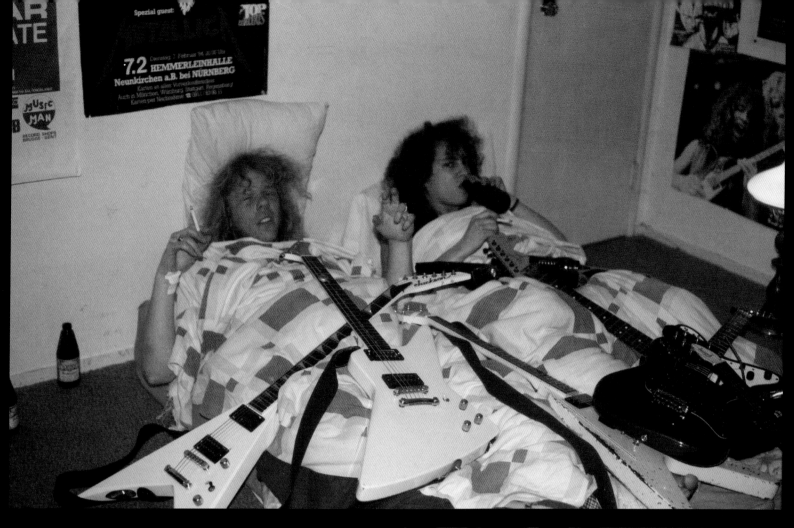

From top: *Hetfield and Kirk Hammett make for strange bedfellows during another of the most memorable impromptu Metalli-shoots, Kirk Hammett's mom's house, El Sobrante.* HARALD OIMOEN; *James in the kitchen at home with producer Mark Whitaker's beloved dog, Clive.* HARALD OIMOEN. Following page: *Ron Quintana used one of these shots for the cover of* Metal Mania, *but he cut out El Duce's fat head and placed it in bed to simulate Jaymz and Kirk sleeping with him. James got pissed off and threatened to never let me take photos of them again.* HARALD OIMOEN

223

Metallica, Metallica Mansion, El Cerrito. I took this series of pics after a killer rehearsal in their garage. I had to cut the proceedings short to head off to a Megadeth show in SF later that night. After I told them that, in the last shot I asked them to all give me the finger and they happily obliged. HARALD OIMOEN. **Overleaf:** *My favorite Metallica photo. I was inspired by an Iron Maiden picture in Kerrang! taken by some asshole English photographer.* HARALD OIMOEN

Above: *Kirk Hammett collapses under the weight of a heavy share of beer.* HARALD OIMOEN.

Facing page, from top: *James Hetfield.* HARALD OIMOEN; *James Hetfield with a Virginia Slim and ex–Anvil Chorus bassist Bill Skinner, Ruthie's Inn.* HARALD OIMOEN

Following page: *Early Metallica secrets revealed! The band were users of matching yellow toothbrushes!* HARALD OIMOEN

After following page: *James Hetfield writing Master of Puppets at home.* HARALD OIMOEN

Both at left: *James Hetfield, Ruthie's Inn.* HARALD OIMOEN. Both at right: *Two of Hetfield's proudest T-shirts. The Alcoholica tee was created by a fan.* HARALD OIMOEN; Facing page: *Lars Ulrich makes heavy breakfast after a long night.* HARALD OIMOEN

From top: *Dave Mustaine, a bad influence on Paul Baloff?* HARALD OIMOEN; *Debbie Abono, tapping some Old English 800 malt liquor, obviously spending too much time around poor young metalheads!* HARALD OIMOEN

Top: *Dave Ellefson, Megadeth manager Jay Jones, and Dave Mustaine appear to stumble into a lesbian make-out session backstage at Ruthie's Inn, due to an accidental double exposure.* HARALD OIMOEN.
Bottom three photos: *Savatage arrive in SF and become honorary Bay Area brethren.* HARALD OIMOEN

Above: *James Hetfield, well into a night of heavy drinking.* HARALD OIMOEN

Facing page, from top: *Cliff and James.* HARALD OIMOEN *Necromancer Cliff and pissy James, men's room of Ruthie's Inn.* HARALD OIMOEN

Preceding pages, above, and facing page: *Metallica, Day on the Green, Oakland, August 31, 1985. Cliff was amazing at this show, and played with an intensity that even surpassed his previously demonstrated brutality. The above shot captures him expelling an epic foot-long loogie.* HARALD OIMOEN

From top: *Cliff Burton and longtime girlfriend Corinne Lynne entering Ruthie's Inn.* HARALD OIMOEN; *Burton and Baloff, two of the Bay Area scene's most beloved characters, both of whom lived and breathed heavy 24 hours a day.* HARALD OIMOEN. Facing page: *Cliff Burton.* HARALD OIMOEN. Overleaf: *Cliff Burton, a boy and his car.* HARALD OIMOEN.

Above negative strip, left to right: 1. *I ran into Cliff and his lovely girl Corinne entering Ruthie's, and ambushed him with a total barrage of strong flashes.* HARALD OIMOEN;
2. *Humorously annoyed, Corinne and Cliff laughed as Cliff grabbed my camera and flashed me back.* HARALD OIMOEN; 3. *"There! See how you fuckin' like it!"* CLIFFORD LEE BURTON.

Above: *Cliff, Mabuhay Gardens, July 20, 1984.* HARALD OIMOEN.
Facing page: *Cliff at the Keystone Palo Alto, Halloween 1983.* HARALD OIMOEN

I CAN STILL FEEL THE THUMP

by Alex Skolnick

I can still feel the thump of the kick, snare, and bass drums, shattering sonic thresholds; a volume so thunderous it would be matched only by the lasting hum in your ears afterward. I can still smell the overwhelming odor of sweat, mixed with that of the occasional can of hair spray (worn strictly by females, contrary to what was going on in L.A. at the time). I still see the pulsating mass of swinging arms, necks, and hair, amidst the ocean of hundreds of bouncing bodies, crowd surfers, and stage divers. And I can still taste the watered-down drinks in plastic cups: cheap vodka, lime juice, and triple sec, appropriately named the kamikaze.

The Omni was a bit like purgatory; the perfect middle ground for Bay Area metal, somewhere between the seedy underworld of Ruthie's Inn and the respectable, established rooms like the Warfield or the Fillmore. A ballroom-style venue, the Omni had a capacity of well over five hundred, and its first-rate sound system was leagues ahead of Ruthie's or the Berkeley Square's. Yet somehow the Omni maintained the vibe of those smaller clubs. This was helped by the fact that there were several bars in the venue, any of which could become territory for friends to converge—including a separate, upstairs bar where you could hear yourself talk and not lose the music; perfect for a quick drink and a few minutes of refuge from the pit.

The Omni was a bit like hell, too, strictly in the following sense: it was blazingly hot. Even those of us who by that time had played in places like Atlanta and Dallas had never experienced anything quite like it. The venue was designed with no cross-ventilation. Throw in a capacity crowd, and you were talking sweat lodge. Add to that the accusation (backed up by more than one reliable source) that, in an attempt to increase the bar profits, the Omni's upper management cranked up the thermostats during sold-out shows. If you were a relatively new, unsigned group—as my band Legacy was in 1985—you got started at Ruthie's Inn,

the unofficial training ground. Until Ruthie's, the next-level club in the East Bay had been the Keystone Berkeley (sister club of the Stone in San Francisco). As an adolescent, I had been sneaking in there for years (often by carrying an amp head or speaker cabinet for Exodus or Laaz Rockit). I was beyond disappointed when the Keystone closed their doors before I ever had a chance to play there. By the time my band, now called Testament, had a record deal, the Omni had come around to replace the Keystone as the East Bay's midlevel club for local and national acts. For the next few years, we played some of our most memorable gigs at the Omni.

The Omni had a sense of danger about it. It was located in the Temescal area of Oakland, considered very sketchy at the time, but which has since become very hip. Several of my friends had stories of being mugged, assaulted, or narrowly escaping one or the other while en route to or from Omni gigs. There was danger on the inside, as well; illegal substances flowed, alcohol abuse abounded, and there would occasionally be a bloody fight, usually broken up quickly by the club's effective security team. But any dark side of the Omni was transcended by something incredibly positive: the coming together of a diverse people for the appreciation of great metal music.

As a performer and an audience member, I will never forget the shows at the Omni. In addition to being the top rock club in the East Bay during the late '80s and early '90s, it became the core of a unique community built around heavy music—a subculture of young, underrepresented, and underestimated Bay Area residents who now finally had an established, respectable venue where their voices could be collectively heard at an excruciating volume.

From top: *Chuck Billy of Testament, the Stone.* HARALD OIMOEN; *Alex Skolnick of Testament, a criminally underrated guitarist who stomps all over certain Big Four lead players, the Stone.* HARALD OIMOEN

Clockwise from top: *Testament show off their new matching tattoos outside their studio off Telegraph Ave., Oakland.* HARALD OIMOEN; *Always ready with a bird, Chuck Billy of Testament, the Omni, 1988.* HARALD OIMOEN; *Steve "Zetro" Souza of Legacy and Chuck "Charles William" Billy of Testament.* HARALD OIMOEN

Facing page: *Chuck Billy onstage with Testament.* HARALD OIMOEN.

Above: *Testament in full-on full-stage mode, Warfield Theatre, SF, May 6, 1990.* HARALD OIMOEN

Clockwise from top: *Vio-lence opening for Spastik Children, Rock on Broadway, January 2, 1987.* HARALD OIMOEN; *Deen Dell of Vio-lence.*

HARALD OIMOEN; *Craig Locicero of Forbidden and Robb Flynn of Vio-lence.* HARALD OIMOEN

Clockwise from top: *Benefit for Andy Galeon of Death Angel following his near-fatal 1990 auto accident. Pictured are members of Death Angel, Metallica, Forbidden, Heathen, Defiance, Debbie Abono, and other friends and family.* HARALD OIMOEN *Andy Galeon.* HARALD OIMOEN *Death Angel in their rehearsal studio, Hayward.* HARALD OIMOEN

Clockwise from top: *Blind Illusion takes a shower, left to right: Larry LaLonde, Les Claypool, Marc Biedermann, Mike Miner.* HARALD OIMOEN;

Les Claypool onstage with "Blind L," the Stone. HARALD OIMOEN; *Testament's Greg Christian and Primus's Les Claypool.* HARALD OIMOEN;

Kirk Hammett joins his high school pal Les Claypool of Primus onstage. HARALD OIMOEN

Clockwise from top: *Gwar invades San Francisco.* HARALD OIMOEN; *Pantera finds their new level.* HARALD OIMOEN;

Oderus Urungus of Gwar prepares to stuff Jello Biafra into a meat grinder. HARALD OIMOEN

From left: Paul Baloff out shopping; HARALD OIMOEN; *Slayer reigning on the big stage.* HARALD OIMOEN; Below: *As Toby Rage licks Kerry King's shaved head, Jeff Hanneman and Gary Holt wave good-bye, and Robb Flynn's right eyeball and headband slip into view.* HARALD OIMOEN

SOMETIME IN THE '80S IN SAN FRANCISCO

by Robb Flynn

Sometime in the '80s in San Francisco, my friend Jim Pittman, who I credit for getting me into underground metal, and I rode a BART train to the Stone to see one of our favorite bands, Canada's Exciter, who had made an incredible proto-thrash album called *Heavy Metal Maniac*. We went up front to watch Griffin, local also-rans who were unfortunately stuck somewhere between NWOBHM and the young but burgeoning thrash scene. They were not doing either very well, but their roadie made an indelible imprint on our sixteen-year-old brains when he leapt offstage and punched a guy directly in front of me who was heckling and flipping the band off for "not playing fast enough." Whoa! So this was thrash? This was crazy!

(As it turns out, my future partner in crime in Vio-lence and Machine Head, Phil Demmel, was standing right behind me when the punch landed—though we did not meet until a couple years later.)

Exciter took the stage, and Jim and I stayed in front until they began to play, at which point all hell broke loose. A huge, violent circle pit exploded. Though it's hard to believe now, that was an unknown and completely foreign phenomenon. We rushed to the left side of the stage and clawed our way to the very front so we could be in front of my guitar god John Ricci, whose lead in the epic "Cry of the Banshee" was the fastest fucking thing I had heard in my life. We headbanged for the whole show, only occasionally looking up to see a lead or scream a lyric.

By the time it was over, my life would be changed forever. We were supposed to leave early to catch our BART train back, but fuck that, who could concern themselves with something as unimportant as getting home when the metal was still flowing so heavily through our veins? For five hours, we waited outside the closed BART station with two other metalheads, soaked with sweat, ears still ringing, thrilled and roaring/singing lyrics to each other, sharing how fucking incredible the night was. Finally, at 6 a.m., the BART station reopened and we said our good-byes to our new metal brothers. And so began my journey into the world of thrash, punk, and metal.

Every Saturday night at 2 a.m., Jim and I began taping Ron Quintana's *Rampage Radio* on KUSF with my small RadioShack tape deck/radio combo. We had to stand in a certain room in my house, aiming the antenna toward the University of San Francisco in just the right way, or the whole thing turned to static. There we discovered even more thrash and punk, and each week's show became the bible from which we learned. Jim soon began trading tapes with other traders, collecting bootlegs, albums, and demos, and quickly amassing a fourteen-page list of the most coveted underground music around.

I went to see D.R.I. at the Mabuhay Gardens. At the time, D.R.I.'s fans were mainly the SF Skins, a local skinhead gang with a serious penchant for beating the shit out of anyone with hair, which unfortunately my friend Leroy and I had down to our shoulders. We stood terrified as we watched their *humongous* leader, "Dagger," knock a long-haired guy out at the front door, exclaiming for nobody in particular to hear: "NO LONGHAIRS!" D.R.I. were vicious, unrelenting, fast, and frankly psychotic, as they played to about 150 guy and girl skinheads who were literally beating themselves bloody.

I also saw Raven, Metallica, and Exodus at the Berkeley Keystone on the Kill 'Em All for One tour. I had my dad drop Jim and me off a couple blocks away, so no one would think we were posers, and we actually got an autograph from James Hetfield, who was signing stuff in the crowd before the show. Exodus were great but had a considerable number of technical problems, the biggest being drummer Tom Hunting's cymbal stands, which were hanging off of the extremely small stage and had to be held up from the front by a roadie and other headbanging fans for the entire show. As you might imagine, that made for a lot of moving cymbals. Metallica were amazing—life changing. We sang every word, banged, screamed, and dreamed. Raven were great too, an incredible live band, but we had to leave early as my dad was picking us up, and, of course, as young sixteen-year-old thrashers, we couldn't let anyone see that.

Robb Flynn, the Omni, sometime in the '80s. HARALD OIMOEN

That night on the drive home Jim and I decided that we *had* to start a thrash band. He had a drum kit already, and we had jammed a few times, but this was more serious. He told me: "You need to get better on guitar *right now*." We chose our set list that night: Metallica, "Whiplash" (and, well, anything off *Kill 'Em All*); Exodus, "Bonded by Blood" and "A Lesson in Violence"; Accept, "Fast as a Shark"; and other songs by Holocaust, Witchfinder General, Priest, Maiden, Sabbath, D.R.I., and whatever else we could figure out. For a brief time, we practiced in our bassist Steve Lombardo's parents' garage, learning how to be a band and play together. Later, my dad let us practice in our garage, and after that the living room. By that point we were frequently skipping high school from second period through lunch, with all sorts of people coming over to have various jams, all while my dad was at work, unaware. The first solo I ever learned how to play was Gary Holt's lead in "Bonded by Blood." The first riff I learned to play on guitar while singing at the same time was the bridge in Metallica's "Trapped Under Ice": *"Scream, from my soul, fate mystified, hell forever more."*

I became totally obsessed. I would see a guy with a Slayer shirt at the bus stop, and it was like: "I know you . . . we're the same." I punched a kid and broke his nose at an

Anthrax show at the Kabuki for saying Gary Holt sucked. Yes, I was a thrasher, willing to fight and bang and bleed for my thrash metal gods.

Soon our band was playing backyard parties, church halls, community centers, and people's living rooms. We were an unsigned band with only some rehearsal tapes recorded on a boom box, but we pulled a lot of kids at a rec hall. Something was really happening then, a buzz that spread even to the suburbs of Fremont, California, where I lived, fifty miles outside of San Francisco. It was an incredible time. It was violent, it was dangerous, it was drug- and alcohol-fueled, you had to learn to tell the wolves from the sheep, and girls suddenly thought I was cool. I became completely and utterly enamored with this world. We had no idea that moment was so special, happening right here in our own backyard. That moment would go on to change the face of music as we know it, and defined a generation—posers and thrashers—so clear, so simple, so ignorantly defined. Our musical leaders captured the fears of teenagers growing up in the nuclear age, harnessed the hearts of the rebellious, and taught us to "fight! For what you believe to be right! Crush it with all your might!" That is the moment that we now know as . . . *thrash metal.*

JANA PERRY

San Francisco Bay Area native Harald Oimoen has never grown up, and never plans to. His conservative traditional parents want him to settle down and get a real job—but it ain't gonna happen. He is still active in the local music scene and enjoys going to metal gigs. When not touring the world playing bass for semi-legendary punk metallers D.R.I. (Dirty Rotten Imbeciles), he works security for N.E.S. and the legendary Fillmore nightclub. He enjoys collecting all varieties of crap, including: trading cards, guitar picks, weird toys., horror movie crap, *Simpsons* crap, and tons of other crap! Harald is a true free spirit who follows his own path, regardless of common sense or current trends. He is already digging through his endless avalanche of negatives to piece together *MITFR 2: More Murder in the Front Row*.

His photos appear on many albums, including Metallica's *Ride the Lightning*, Exodus's *Bonded by Blood*, Slayer's *Hell Awaits*, Possessed's *Seven Churches*, Machine Head's *Burn My Eyes*, Megadeth's *Killing Is My Business…* reissue; in the books *Mustaine*, by Dave Mustaine, *Metallica Unbound*, by K.J. Doughton, *So What! The Official Metallica Illustrated Chronicles*, edited by Steffan Chirazi; and in many, many magazines and TV productions including *MTV Behind the Music: Metallica*, *A&E Biography: Metallica*, and *MTV Icon: Metallica*.

Thanks to the following amazing human beings who have made my quest for world metal photo domination much easier:

My partners-in-crime and true metal brothers Brian and Ian! You've made this the funnest, most stress-free project I've ever been involved with, and I'm proud to call you best friends! Here's to many happy future collaborations.

My fantastic parents Kari and Bud for making me possible, and for raising me in the fertile metal soil of the SF Bay Area so I could grow up to put out this book.

My fellow bandmates in D.R.I.—the last thirteen years have been a blast. Thank you for giving me the chance to live out my dream.

And James, Lars, Kirk, Vickie Strate, Steffan Chirazi and Toby at MetClub, Big Mick Hughes, Corinne Lynn, Joel McIver and *Bass Guitar*, Jim "Fatso" Martin, Mike Wasco, Lorraine and Jeff Brenner, Karl Casolari, Mike Smario, Jeff Nix, Greg Lee, Ron Quintana, Rissa Schiff, Bill Graham, Leah Storkson, Jason Newsted, Dave Mustaine, Dave "Jr." Ellefson, Greg Davis, Steve "Zet" Souza, Phil Demmel, Bill Hale, Satan, Bootleg Bob Reynolds, Jim King, Tiffany and Chuck Billy, Greggy Christian, Alan Ralph, Craig and Pam Behrhorst, Johnny Araya, Lonn Friend, Dave Lombardo, Kerry King, Tom Araya, Jeff Hanneman, Alex Skolnick, Kurt Brecht, Spike and Jana Cassidy, Rob Rampy and "Dude", Tor and Berit Bang, Mark Peterson, Chris and Greg Hoff, Homer and Bart Simpson, Tony, Debra, and Jason at the Fillmore, Larry at the Warfield, Leo and Gabe, Dennis and Ian King, Rob Sample, *Mad*, Eric Reed, Mike Muir, Ventor and Mille from Kreator, Joey Houston, Chris Kontos, Gwynne Coffee, Alfred E. Newman, Mike Judge, Rush, Mikey Porter, the Porter family, Mark Alden, "Metal" Maria Ferrero and Adrenaline PR, Al Luchessi, Dave Lopez, Larry David, Gary Holt, Robb and Genevra Flynn, Deen, Dave, and Judy Dell, Andy Dick, Walter Morgan, Matt Groening, Terry Brewster, Russ Brigham, Phil Sedgly, Jeff Weller, Fred Cotton, Brian Slagel, *Revolver*, *Guitar World*, K.J. Doughton, Issues, and YOU for buying this book!

Thanks to all the bands I have ever photographed, all the clubs that let me shoot, all the cool folks in the SF metal scene, all the people I've met on the road with DRI, and all my friends in the digital land. You know who you are!

Special extra cool thanks to Roadrunner honcho and all-around good guy Monte Conner for suggesting Bazillion Points and hooking me up with Ian Christe and his fine publishing company (the perfect publisher for this project!)

BRIAN LEW

Born and raised in the San Francisco Bay Area, Brian first discovered European metal in the import bins of Tower Records in the early '80s, and Motörhead and Iron Maiden changed his life. While in high school, he started taking concert photos and contributing to Ron Quintana's legendary San Francisco fanzine *Metal Mania*. Brian later put out the fanzine *Whiplash* with the late Sam Kress. He once had his glasses broken in the pit during an Exodus show at Ruthie's Inn. He will argue forever that it was the bullshit hair metal bands that destroyed '80s metal—not grunge. In recent years, Brian has worked in the music and entertainment merchandise business. Happily many of his present clients are the real metal bands that were his metal

Brad Schmidt, Steven Cuevas, Walt Rogers, Ken Mitolo, Andy Anderson, Chris Scaparro, Cristie Carter, Rick Strahl, Hans Bruhner, Doug Piercy, Dalia Zatkin, Tim Healy, John Marshall, Bob Nalbandian, Dana Schecter, Mark Paschke, Leah Storkson, Corinne Lynn, Erik Lannon, Tracey Rayfield, Craig and Pam Behrhorst, Dave Quon, Mark DeVito, Rebecca Kestelyn, Laura Stewart, Tom Christie, Lisa Perticone, Gary Holt, Raymond Ahner, Cynthia Poon, Sven Soderlund, William Howell, Ron McGovney, Dave and Sheila Marrs, Brian Ross, "Metal" Mike van Rijswijk, Bernard Doe, Alex Gernandt, Brian Slagel, Steffan Chirazi, Micki Mihich, Hans Haedelt, Tom Trakas, Timothy Bold, the Record Vault (Zary, Pam, and Greg), and that pimply-faced band Metallica (Lars, James,

RAYMOND AHNER

Postcard, February 7, 1984: *"I'd rather have a bottle in front of me, than a frontal lobotomy! Hello Fellow Freaks! Having a fuckin' blast! I'm sitting on the Metallibus watching Richard Pryor on video (WOW!). Styling bus, 8 bunks, bar, jacuzzi, sauna, and tennis court on roof! We're on our way to the gig in Nürnberg. We had to sleep over in Munich 'cause we couldn't find a hotel in Nürnberg because of some toy makers convention or some shit. The first gig in Zurich, Switzerland was o.k. but no soundcheck about 800 people. 2nd gig in Milano, Italy was great, about 1,500 crazy Italian Metallithrashers. Gigs are getting better, we're going down better than Venom. I think their show is good but their boring music shows through. We've got about 20 lights and that's all. Booze is great here. Sick dark beers! How about sending some new issues to Sweet Silence around February 20 when we start recording Ride The Lightning. We saw Accept at Hammersmith was good and Hellion at Marquee they suck. AARGH, James."*

Postcard, June 1984: *"Yo, so how are things back there! Just finished the new album yesterday and it's nice to finally be thru with that and get out and play live again. Apart from the Venom tour we only done the Marquee twice so the mini tour we are about to do will be fuckin' great. Around 6 dates with T. Sister (who?)+ the big festival in Belgium with Motörhead, Twisted Sister, Manowank, Fate, etc. Europe will be destroyed Part 2. AARRRGGHH! Hangin' out with Mercyful Fate alot. Great fuckin' guys!! They are doin' their new album right now too by the way. Thanks alot for the tapes and shit back in Feb. See you soon. Lars. Drink & destroy."*

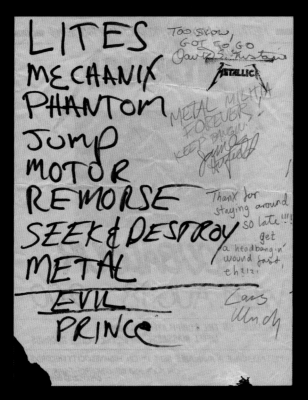

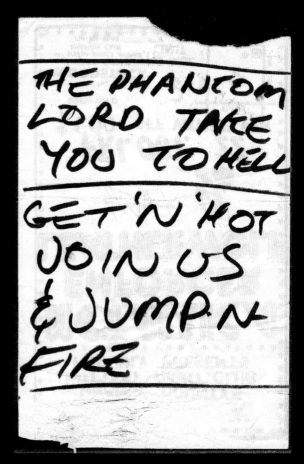

From left: *Metallica setlist from their first San Francisco show, the Stone, September 18, 1982. The band autographed it after the show—except Ron McGovney, I don't remember why not!* BRIAN LEW; *Metallica stage banter cue card, the Old Waldorf, San Francisco, October 18, 1982.* BRIAN LEW

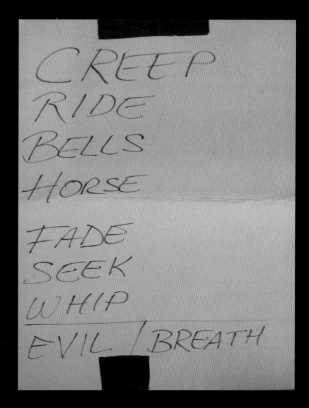

From left: *Letter from Lars, December 1982. The "live tape" was the* Metal Up Your Ass *live demo. Note that Lars asked for my negatives, and he probably still has them!* BRIAN LEW; *Metallica setlist from Day On The Green, Oakland Stadium, August 31, 1985.* JOHN MARSHALL

8-24-84

HARED (struck through)

HAROLD! (FUCK!!!)

THOSE PIX ARE GREAT.!!!...

WE COULDN'T GET "JAY JONES",
OUR MANAGER......TO GIVE UP A SHIRT
SO ME & DAVE JUST GAVE YOU ONE
OF THE ONES THAT WE HAD. (I KNOW
IT'S NOT NEW, BUT YOU'LL SEE WHAT A
JERK JAY IS WHEN WE COME UP)
    PLEASE NUMBER YOUR PIX SO WE
CAN REORDER IN A SENSIBLE WAY.
I NEED TO HAVE THE WHOLE PORTFOLIO
YOU HAVE ON US, AND YES YOU ARE
GETTING CREDIT FOR YOUR PHOTOS,
SO I'M SURE YOU'LL BENEFIT FROM
SENDING A FEW PIX FOR BOTH OF OUR
PROMO. WE GIVE YOU A "NEW" SHIRT
WHEN WE PLAY UP THERE ON HALLOWEEN
                            MUSTAINE

Dave Mustaine letter: "Those pix are great!!!... Please number your pix so we can reorder in a sensible way..." HARALD OIMOEN